INTERNAT[IONAL]
SOCIALIS[M]
A quarterly journal of s[ocialist theory]

CW00725008

Autumn 1995

Contents

Issue 68 of INTERNATIONAL SOCIALISM, quarterly journal of the Socialist Workers Party (Britain)

Published September 1995
Copyright © International Socialism
Distribution/subscriptions: International Socialism,
PO Box 82, London E3.
American distribution: B de Boer, 113 East Center St, Nutley,
New Jersey 07110.
Subscriptions and back copies: PO Box 16085, Chicago
Illinois 60616
Editorial and production: 0171 538 1626/0171 538 0538
Sales and subscriptions: 0171 538 5821
American sales: 312 665 7337

ISBN 189 88 761 0X

Printed by BPCC Wheatons Ltd, Exeter, England
Typeset by East End Offset, London E3

Cover design by Mark Bell

For details of back copies see the end pages of this book

Subscription rates for one year (four issues) are:

Britain and overseas (surface):	individual	£14.00 ($30)
	institutional	£25.00
Air speeded supplement:	North America	nil
	Europe/South America	£2.00
	elsewhere	£4.00

Note to contributors

The deadline for articles intended for issue 71 of *International Socialism* is 1 December 1995.

All contributions should be double spaced with wide margins. Please submit two copies. If you write your contribution using a computer, please also supply a disk, together with details of the computer and programme used.

INTERNATIONAL SOCIALISM ★

A quarterly journal of socialist theory

RACISM AND IMMIGRATION controls are two stock responses for any unpopular Tory government. Britain's current Conservative administration is no exception—the latest in a long line of racist legislation aimed at immigrants is due on the statute books this autumn. Ruth Brown looks at the history of immigration controls, charts their intimate connection with the capitalist system's need for labour power and details the role of the Labour Party in allowing the political agenda to be determined by the racist right.

JOHN MOLYNEUX takes issue with one of the most common accusations levelled at Marxism—that it is a deterministic theory which leaves little room for conscious human action. He shows the extent to which Marx and his inheritors have tried to explain the working of society by analysing its economic and social structure, but he also demonstrates how much the Marxist tradition has given to the age old desire to shape the world according to human needs and wants.

STUART HOOD is both a veteran of the BBC and author of the widely read *On Television.* Here he reviews part of a new *History of Broadcasting.* Lee Sustar reviews a history of the US Communist Party while fellow American socialist, Peter Linebaugh, author of *The London Hanged,* reviews V A C Gatrell's *The Hanging Tree.* Our reviews are concluded with George Paizis's look at Alex Callinicos's new book, *Theories and Narratives.*

CHRIS HARMAN'S 'The Prophet and the Proletariat' in *International Socialism* 64 has drawn a comment on Islam from Phil Marshall.

THE CENTENARY of cinema provides Paul D'Amato with the chance to recommend some of the best books on the movies in this quarter's *Bookwatch.*

Editor: John Rees. Assistant Editors: Alex Callinicos, Chris Harman, John Molyneux, Lindsey German, Ann Rogers, Colin Sparks, Mike Gonzalez, Peter Morgan, Ruth Brown, Mike Haynes, Judy Cox and Rob Hoveman.

Racism and immigration in Britain

RUTH BROWN

The recent deaths of Joy Gardner and Joseph Nnalue during attempts to deport them have highlighted the desperate plight of those who seek refuge in Britain today. Across Western Europe and the US, politicians have reached a consensus that immigrants from poorer countries can be blamed for bad housing and unemployment. Opposition to immigration has become the rallying cry of all right wing politicians, of racists and of Nazi parties. Wherever tighter immigration controls have more or less prevented all primary immigration, the focus has turned increasingly to refugees and to the dependents of immigrants. In California Order 187 seeks to deny healthcare and education to the children of 'illegal' immigrants. Ominously, advisers to the right wing of the Tory party have been studying these proposals with great interest. In Britain only a handful of immigrants can legally enter Britain. Some are married to British citizens and some are, quite simply, rich. Thus to prove they are 'tough' on immigrants the Tory cabinet will introduce new laws on illegal immigrants this autumn, possibly involving identity cards. This is despite the fact that the number of illegal immigrants in Britain appears to be shrinking and there has never been any evidence that illegal immigrants put any extra strain on services.

Whatever the hard facts, the need for immigration controls is widely accepted. The tabloid press is very fond of scare stories about immigrants 'fiddling' the benefits system. The fact that Labour Party and trade union leaders have always supported immigration controls means that racist ideas about immigration can sometimes gain a hearing among workers. Central to much racist ideology about immigration into Britain is the notion that immigration is a very recent phenomenon, which began only with the arrival of black workers from the Caribbean and the Indian sub-continent in the 1950s and 1960s. This view rests on the assumption that the British nation and the 'British character' were developed, throughout history, in splendid isolation from the rest of the world, untainted by unwelcome contact or exchange with 'foreigners' or 'outsiders'.

This view of immigration depends on a deliberate rewriting of history. It is a version of the past which excludes not only all black people, but most other 'non-British' nationalities from the history of civilisation in what is now called Britain. In fact, the population of Britain has always been composed of different peoples. The Celts, Saxons and Vikings all came to Britain as the result of various invasions, making the British the most ethnically composite of all European peoples.[1]

But in pre-capitalist societies the number of people who moved across different territories—or even significant distances within one geographical area—remained very small, and usually involved only traders and merchants. Large scale movements of people in search of work are unique to modern capitalism, and immigration as we understand it today really began in the 19th century with the consolidation of unified nation states with recognisable borders. Immigration went hand in hand with the development of the capitalist system and the capitalist state. In its earliest years this took the form of the slave trade, the first large scale forced movement of labour in history. As Marx put it, 'the veiled slavery of the wage workers in Europe needed for its pedestal slavery pure and simple'.[2] Virtually every section of British capitalism relied on the massive wealth which derived from the slave trade to get a head start over its competitors. Britain's key role in the forced transportation of some 30 million black people between 1500 and 1800 illustrates much more than the sheer cruelty of Britain's capitalist class—it also represents the first organised attempt by British capitalists to meet the insatiable demand for labour which characterised early capitalism.

The development of capitalism depended not only on slavery, but also on the free movement of labour. The migration of labour has always reflected the combined and uneven development of capitalism on a global level. Workers follow capital to the most developed areas to meet the demand for wage labour in urban centres of capitalist expansion. In the process they attempt to escape poverty and unemployment in areas where capitalism is in decline, or where it has failed to take off altogether. This is a process which frequently takes place within the boundaries of a country, but modern capitalism is also characterised by large scale movements of workers across the borders of individual nation states. Just as capital is moved from one geographical area to another, in search of the most profitable location, so too labour, with greater difficulty, moves after it. In 19th century Britain, for example, many who moved to work in the cotton mills were escaping the effects of the enclosure of the land.[3] But by the mid-19th century huge numbers of Irish people were forced by famine in Ireland to join them, working on the railways, the docks and the mills in appalling conditions.[4]

It was the development of railways and steamships which made both internal and external migration an option for thousands of people. By 1840 approximately 70,000 people were emigrating from Britain every year and in the mid-1850s this number doubled after the discovery of gold in California. Most went to British 'commonwealth' colonies, like Canada, Australia and New Zealand and, increasingly, to the US. By 1871 Britain had become a net exporter of population. *With only a few notable exceptions, this has continued to be the case throughout each successive decade of the 20th century.* Capitalism has made immigration both possible and also necessary, as the system has historically depended on the labour which immigration makes available.[5]

Throughout the 19th century mass immigration transformed whole countries, the most dramatic example being America. In half a century America was transformed from an insignificant nation on the periphery of Europe into the most populous nation in the Western world, with historically unprecedented levels of immigration called forth by and fuelling huge levels of economic growth. Even so the 'American dream' did not become a reality for most immigrant workers who faced poverty and discrimination. Throughout the 19th century cities with the largest immigrant populations were the poorest of all—in 1860 the death rate in New York was twice as high as that of London. As early as 1840 in the largest American cities, the richest 5 percent of the population owned 70 percent of all property and by 1860 the richest 5 percent of adult males owned 53 percent of all wealth, whilst only 1 percent was owned by the poorest half of the population.[6]

Patterns of early immigration into the US demonstrate how immigration is closely related to the level of demand for labour in the American economy, as well as to job prospects in the immigrant worker's country of origin. Though many went to the US to escape from persecution, such as the Jews who fled from pogroms in Eastern Europe, the basic link between immigration and the availability of jobs (both in the 'host' country and at home) remains central. This is not only true of the US. In Britain large scale emigration continued unabated, particularly from the 1870s onwards, as British capitalism began to enter into a period of economic decline. [7]

Even so Britain also continued to import labour throughout the 19th century and it was invariably those groups moving into—rather than out of—Britain who attracted the most attention, especially Irish immigrants and, from the 1880s, Jews from Eastern Europe. Economic destitution and vicious persecution combined to drive huge numbers of workers westwards at the end of the century, and a significant proportion of these headed for Britain, often en route to the US.

The 1905 Aliens Act

In keeping with its role as the 'workshop of the world', Britain long enjoyed a reputation as a liberal provider of refuge and political asylum. The British ruling class had little use for immigration controls for most of the 19th century. The 'free' approach to immigration flourished in the heyday of free trade, as British capitalism expanded to the four corners of the globe. During the boom years of the industrial revolution British capitalism lapped up labour with an insatiable thirst, if only to throw workers back into unemployment in times of slump. Britain's bosses showed little interest in the national or ethnic 'character' of the labour power which they sucked into the expanding British economy.

However, by the turn of the century Britain clearly no longer 'ruled the waves', its industry increasingly undermined by cheaper imports from abroad. The end of the 19th century was marked by deep economic depression and political crises, as huge price rises led to massive cuts in virtually all workers' standards of living, and rising unemployment forced millions into abject poverty. The working class responded with the explosion of 'new unionism', embodied in the strike wave which swept Britain in 1889, involving thousands of women and immigrant workers.

Sadly, the heroic struggles which characterised this period of 'new unionism' proved to be shortlived. The ruling class fought back, and against the background of working class defeat the first law aimed at controlling immigration into Britain was introduced. The 1905 Aliens Act introduced by Balfour's Tory government had an overriding advantage for the government and the ruling class as a whole. It institutionalised the idea that immigrants alone were responsible for the rapidly deteriorating conditions which most workers were suffering.

The introduction of the act was accompanied by a rise of anti-semitism, led by the gutter press, against the growing numbers of impoverished Jewish refugees arriving in London's East End. In parliament Tory MPs whipped up an anti-semitic frenzy. One even likened Jewish immigration to the entry of diseased cattle from Canada.[8] Jewish refugees were simultaneously accused of taking British workers' jobs *and* of living on welfare, in the same racist—and self contradictory—mythology which opponents of immigration continue to employ against migrant workers today. Outside parliament backbench Tory MPs were also key to building Britain's first anti-immigrant organisations like the British Brothers League which, for the first time, succeeded in mobilising some level of working class support. Growing unemployment and particularly bad housing conditions in London's East End made newly arrived Jewish immigrants an easy scapegoat.[9]

The official leadership of the British working class movement capitulated to growing racism and anti-semitism within British society, and actually did much to make racism respectable inside parts of the working class movement. The official trade union movement repeatedly blamed immigrant workers for the growing levels of unemployment within the British economy and from 1892 onwards the TUC called for a complete halt to immigration. Meanwhile in London Ben Tillett, the dockers' leader, told migrant workers, 'Yes, you are our brothers, and we will do our duty by you. But we wish you had not come'.[10]

Given the hostility which union leaders and others directed at Jewish migrant workers, it is fairly remarkable that so many of them did consistently refuse to break the ranks of the working class. Strikes like that of the Jewish tailors in Leeds showed the potential which clearly existed for building united working class opposition, not only to the racist agitation which preceded the introduction of the Aliens Act, but also to the growing offensive against working class living standards.[11]

Notwithstanding the overtly racist and anti-semitic character of the agitation which led up to the Aliens Act, it remains essentially a piece of class legislation. Growing competition for jobs within the working class, as well as for other basic necessities of life like housing, was increasingly evident during this period. Both Liberal and Tory politicians attempted to conceal their abject failures by blaming immigrants for the growing housing crisis. As Liberal MP Cathcart Wilson put it, 'What is the use of spending thousands of pounds on building beautiful workmen's dwellings if the places of our own workpeople, the backbone of the country, are to be taken over by the refuse scum of other nations?'[12]

As with all subsequent immigration controls in Britain, the Aliens Act was thus designed primarily to create an easy target for an increasingly impoverished and unemployed working class and marks one of the first institutionalised attempts by the British ruling class to divide and rule the working population by means of overt racism. Of course, it was never clearly stated that the act was aimed only at Jews, but nobody was left in any doubt as to who its intended targets would be. Crucially the act was aimed only at keeping out working class Jews, those 'without visable means of support'.

Immigration between the wars

Once in place, successive governments were more than keen to extend the basic framework of the 1905 Act, despite clear evidence that the Act was not popular. This was increasingly the case as the ruling class faced another rising tide of militancy. By the eve of the First World War workers were spending nearly four times as many days on strike as they had done at the turn of the century. The national dock strike of 1911 was accompanied by the first ever national rail strike and in the following year miners also took national strike action for the first time.

The outbreak of war in 1914 meant that the ruling class was provided with a perfect excuse for renewed attempts to whip up nationalism and jingoism. In August 1914 the Aliens Restriction Act was rushed through parliament virtually unopposed. Some 28,744 Austrians and Germans were instantly repatriated and 32,000 other 'non-British' nationals were interned in prison camps, where they remained for the course of the war.[13] Apart from White Russians fleeing the Russian Revolution, Britain's increasingly rigid immigration controls meant that few others were able to gain entry to Britain during the course of the First World War. The Aliens Restriction Act, combined with the Defence of the Realm Act, passed some weeks later, created for the first time a clear definition of British nationality in law and laid down strict guidelines for local police and military authorities in their treatment of 'aliens'.

The 1919 Aliens Act was introduced against the background of fervent nationalism and anti-German feeling created by the First World War. It formed the basis of all immigration legislation until the introduction of the 1971 Immigration Act, and was renewed every single year between 1919 and 1971. Crucially the 1919 Aliens Act greatly restricted the employment of 'alien' workers in Britain. German and Jewish workers became Tory politicians' most favoured, if not their sole, explanation for the obvious decline of British capitalism. But the Tory party certainly had no monopoly over the growing institutionalisation of racism in British society between the wars. The infant Labour Party did nothing to counter the overtly anti-semitic agitation in which Tory MPs frequently indulged. Although this growing nationalism and racism inside parliament, and amongst at least some sections of British society between the wars, was ultimately a product of the economic depression, the actual levels of labour migration *decreased* dramatically during this period. With no jobs available, there was little motivation for workers to move. Between the 1920s and 1930s there was a staggering decline in the total number of new immigrant workers entering Britain with the figure standing at around 700 a year for most of this period. This was ultimately a result of the almost complete lack of job opportunities in Britain. Although economic conditions were even worse in places like the Caribbean, with whole sections of the economy collapsing with the onset of slump, workers simply sat it out at home, rather than face racism and unemployment in Britain.

Even when Jewish refugees fleeing the rise of Nazism in Austria and Germany began to arrive in Britain during the late 1930s, entry was granted only to a tiny minority of those who promised that they intended to settle permanently elsewhere. MPs complained relentlessly about Jewish refugees 'scurrying' from Germany into Britain and regularly called for a further tightening of controls.[14] Many of those who did manage to gain admission to Britain were then deported within months of arriving, alongside thousands of 'enemy aliens'. Mass deportations continued throughout the Second World War even after a ship carrying a human cargo of mainly Germans, Italians and Austrians, most of whom had lived in Britain for more than 20 years, was torpedoed off the west coast of Ireland causing the deaths of nearly 700.

In 1941 the British government also reintroduced internment and included within its remit literally thousands of Jews who wanted to enlist in the war against Hitler. For those not interned, deportation, mainly to Canada and Australia, was usually their fate. Some estimates put the total number of Jewish refugees from the Holocaust who managed to get into Britain as low as 10,000 during the whole of the Second World War.[15] Many Jews were forced to stay in Germany, or to return there, because the doors of every major Western power were firmly closed in their faces. In this respect the British government helped to play its part, alongside many other European nations, in driving millions of Jews into Hitler's concentration camps during the course of the Second World War.

In sharp contrast, the British government made sure that its restrictions on the entry of Jewish and other refugees did not stop it ignoring the provisions of the Aliens Act when it needed to recruit labour. Given the acute labour shortages which developed in some sections of the British economy, particularly after 1943, it might appear irrational for British capitalism to have continued to rely on this strict system of immigration controls during the Second World War. In fact, throughout the war the British government brought more than 60,000 Irish men and women to work in Britain, as well as smaller numbers from the Caribbean and the Indian sub-continent.[16]

By recruiting labour through state sponsored schemes which, by definition, fell outside the remit of the Aliens Act, the British wartime government thus got the best of both worlds. On the one hand migrant labour could continue to be recruited when needed, directed now by the state towards those areas of the economy where labour shortages were developing. On the other hand the maintenance of the Aliens Act, as well as the introduction of internment and the mass deportations of 'enemy aliens', helped the ruling class to galvanise a growing mood of nationalism and xenophobia at least amongst some sections of the British population. This reinforced the greater involvement of the state in the labour market and in the economy generally, which occurred during and after the Second World War.

Immigration and the post-war boom

None of the major advanced capitalist countries ended the Second World War with a significantly reduced labour force, in spite of the appalling numbers of dead and wounded.[17] By 1946 industrial production in Britain was roughly equal to the level of 1938.[18] Employment levels were slightly higher than in the years immediately preceding the war. Even so it was clearly recognised by Britain's rulers in the immediate post-war years that reconstruction would need an injection of additional labour power, at least in those areas of the economy where backlogs of neglected work existed, especially after women were initially encouraged to leave wartime industries and go back to the home.

Rising fears of future labour shortages in the British economy thus lay behind the Labour government's liberal policy towards 'enemy' prisoners and expatriates from 1946 onwards, and were also responsible for a significant number of state directed schemes aimed at encouraging the settlement of 'foreign' workers in Britain immediately after the war. Plans to repatriate thousands of Poles were shelved in 1946, for strictly practical, not humanitarian, reasons.[19] And Labour quickly reversed its initial post-war policy of pushing women workers out of the workforce when in 1947 it broadcast radio appeals for women to re-enter the workforce.

Within only a few years of closing its doors to the victims of the Holocaust, Britain thus introduced a 'positive' immigration policy, whereby it again organised state sponsored recruitment schemes outside the terms of the Aliens Act. Unfortunately, this enthusiasm extended only to healthy able bodied workers. Those brought to Britain under the schemes were liable to deportation if they fell ill—one young boy, who lost an eye at work after falling off a lorry in a farming accident, was actually deported back to Germany. Indeed, Britain's treatment of displaced persons and refugees after the war was so disgraceful that even the United Nations accused Britain of subjecting its newly arrived workers to 'an official policy of discrimination'.[20]

A report from the Royal Commission on Population, published in 1949, recommended that immigration into Britain should be welcomed 'without reserve' but only on the condition that the migrants were 'of good stock and were not prevented by their race or religion from intermarrying with the host population and becoming merged into it'.[21] This referred to the arrival of the *SS Empire Windrush* in Britain the previous year, which had brought some 400 West Indians to Britain in search of work. The commission broadly hinted in the report that 'coloured' immigration would not provide a satisfactory solution to Britain's future labour shortages. Even so during the 1950s employers would prove to be far less concerned about religion or race than with maintaining production whatever the Royal Commission's attitude. British employers were quick to recognise the Caribbean and the Indian sub-continent as fertile recruiting grounds for labour during the 1950s, whatever racist ideas they held. It is interesting to note that some of the most vehement opponents of immigration during the 1960s, such as Tory MP Peter Thorneycroft were actually complaining in the 1950s that immigration controls which prevented 'free men' from coming to Britain were 'contemptible'.[22]

For the capitalist class migrant labour has one central advantage: they have to contribute nothing at all to the cost of raising and educating immigrant workers. This advantage is quickly eroded if immigrant workers bring with them any dependants who are themselves unable to work for reasons of age or health. Family reunion also indicates, of course, a likelihood that the family intends to settle in the 'host' country, thereby creating new demands for the provision of facilities and resources. As early as 1947 the British government abandoned any pretence of concern for the plight of refugees who had been separated from their families by the war and effectively banned the entry of dependants by forcing prospective migrants to sign a form stating that they were single, unattached and had no dependent relatives.[23]

This one single act effectively marked the beginning of a pattern of government legislation which has dominated not only Britain, but most of the advanced capitalist countries, since the 1950s. Aimed at strictly controlling both the level and the nature of immigration, it reflects the need for governments to ensure a continuing supply of flexible labour. And by prohibiting the entry of the family dependants of these 'ready made' workers, the 'host state ensures that it bears little, if any, of the cost of reproducing migrant labour. In the 1950s massive amounts of arms spending stimulated a huge expansion in the economy. Labour shortages were thus a central concern for Western European ruling classes. By the time that the first Tory government since the Second World War was elected, acute labour shortages were its biggest problem, reflected in the King's speech, which spoke of 'serious shortages of labour [which have] handicapped production in a number of industries'.[24]

By the mid-1960s full employment had arrived. Official unemployment was no higher than 3 percent across the advanced economies. In Britain unemployment reached 3 percent during the fuel crisis of the winter of 1947,[25] and remained somewhat lower for the greater part of two decades. By June 1951 there were 3.5 million more workers employed in Britain than there had been at the end of the Second World War and the British economy grew faster than at any time since the peak of the Victorian era, with real wages rising by more than 25 percent between 1952 and 1962.[26] For some, including many on the left of the Labour Party, Keynesianism seemed to have banished mass unemployment forever, and to be transforming the nature of capitalism.[27]

With the boom boosting the advanced industrial centres of the US and Western Europe, the less developed economies in the world system became desperate to include themselves in the process of capital accumulation. Inevitably more and more workers gravitated to the West during the 1950s and 1960s. Here new industries and services continued to spring up throughout the boom, industries which demanded new skills and offered higher wages. Electrical engineering, petro-chemicals, banking, insurance and public services all expanded dramatically during the 1950s and early 1960s and invariably sucked labour from other sections of the economy. Throughout Western Europe labour shortages developed in a number of different areas of the economy, mainly those with the lowest levels of pay and the poorest working conditions, such as textile production, metal manufacture, the building trade, and the catering and health services.[28]

Migrant labour was a far cheaper way of meeting the demand for labour than other alternatives, such as drawing women into the workforce on a significantly increased level. Western governments thus attempted to solve the problem of selective labour shortages by emphatically encouraging labour migration, sometimes by organising state run recruitment schemes, but also by relying on employers to recruit labour directly through private recruitment agencies. Most of the migrant labour power which serviced the older industries of Western Europe during the post-war boom was drawn from countries on the economic periphery of Europe, like Greece, Spain, Turkey, Italy, Yugoslavia, Morocco and Tunisia, but also from the colonial and ex-colonial countries of the major European powers. These were invariably societies whose economies had been ruined by decades of colonial domination. Poverty and unemployment drove many to emigrate.

The long boom created a mass proletarianisation across European society as millions made the long trek from the family farm to the lights of the big city during those years. Yet with chronic underdevelopment and rapid population growth a feature of economic life in the urban areas of these economies too, millions were forced to continue their journey across Europe to the more advanced cities of the West, whilst others simply moved straight from the countryside in their homeland to the urban areas of the West. By the early 1970s around 11 million migrant workers from southern Europe and the colonies were working in the economies of northern and western Europe.[29]

The largest group to come to Britain after the war were Irish workers drawn mainly from the Republic and during the 1950s Irish migration into Britain reached levels not witnessed since the industrial revolution. In one sense this movement was not separate from the long history of Irish immigration into Britain and, as such, was merely a symptom of Britain's age old exploitation and domination of Ireland. Indeed, it was British colonialism which had 'rewarded' Irish workers with the right of unrestricted entry into Britain making Britain the first option for the mainly semi-skilled and unskilled workers who entered during these years.[30]

As well as Irish workers, an average of 16,000 migrant workers from outside the Commonwealth came to Britain each year between 1951 and 1964, but these figures differed quite markedly each year, according to real levels of labour shortage in the British economy.[31] Moreover, by the mid-1960s Britain was rapidly becoming less and less attractive as a source of jobs, particularly for semi-skilled and unskilled workers. *This is most clearly reflected by the simple fact that far more people left the UK than entered it during the 1960s and early 1970s.* Despite the unprecedented levels of growth created by the post-war boom, Britain's economy grew at a slower rate than most of the other advanced Western economies. Indeed, Britain continued to decline as a world power in the post-war years and was forced to give up much of its empire.

Had Britain not been able to draw on a pool of labour in the Commonwealth, the British government might even have been forced to repeal the Aliens Act, to entice more workers to come to Britain in order to meet the continuing demand for labour in certain areas of the economy. As it turned out, the former colonial territories, their economies starved of investment and distorted by the previously insatiable demands of the leading Western nations for raw materials, ensured a continuous flow of labour out of the Caribbean and the Indian sub-continent and into America and Western Europe even after the long boom had reached its peak. Despite the thinly disguised message from the Royal Commission of Populations of 1949, which essentially tried to 'warn off' bosses from recruiting 'coloured' labour, prospective employers in the 1950s had little concern for the skin colour or religion of their new employees. Whatever racist ideas they held were secondary to their need for workers to fill gaps in the labour market by doing the worst jobs. The reason why Britain's employers so enthusiastically recruited workers from the Commonwealth was that they had nowhere else to get them from.

When the 'racialisation' of British politics emerged fully, some years after the arrival of immigrants from the Commonwealth and the Indian sub-continent, it frequently relied upon a deliberate and insidious denial that there was ever an open invitation from Britain's cabinet ministers and employers to come to this country. To demolish all the racist myths used by politicians then and now, in their attempt to construct the notion that Britain has a 'race/immigration' problem, it is usually necessary to start with this one simple, and undeniable, fact: that British capitalists, and some sections of the British state, initiated and actively encouraged large scale emigration to Britain from the Caribbean and Indian sub-continent during the 1950s and 1960s.

Workers from the Caribbean and the Indian sub-continent came to Britain in the 1950s and 1960s for the same reason that has led workers to migrate throughout the history of capitalism: to find work. Moreover, as with all labour migration, levels of immigration from the Caribbean— and later from the Indian sub-continent—at least to begin with, were always strictly related to the level of demand for labour within the British economy. There was only a slight 'delay' at each end of cycle as levels of immigration adjusted to changed economic circumstances in Britain. In 1959, for instance, levels of immigration into Britain from the Caribbean were too low to meet the boom of that year but, in 1961 when the boom started to peter out, figures for immigration were geared to suit the situation a few months earlier and were therefore slightly too high in relation to actual job opportunities in Britain.[32]

Post-war immigration into Britain from the Caribbean was drawn mainly from the very poorest Caribbean islands, where conditions were harshest of all both for rural and urban populations. Yet workers still continued to make the journey to Britain when the certainty of a job existed. A keen awareness of the state of the British labour market existed in the Caribbean and one West Indian migrant into Britain later recalled that 'the *South London Press* could be brought in Hildage's Drugstore, near West Parade, in downtown Kingston, Jamaica...'[33] This knowledge was also built upon by an informal communications network between migrant workers already settled in Britain and friends and acquaintances back home. Individual employers in Britain were often known to exploit this informal network in their efforts to recruit labour, as well as paying for advertisements in New Commonwealth countries. However informal much of this process was, it still proved to be an extremely accurate mechanism for meeting labour demand in Britain and immigration levels consistently dropped very quickly after any drop in the number of advertised vacancies. It was only the racism of Britain's rulers some years later which destroyed this 'natural' relationship between levels of labour migration and the level of demand for labour.

In the early 1960s government ministers, as well as private employers, started to recruit directly in the West Indies. These included Enoch Powell, who actively encouraged the migration of medical staff from India and the West Indies during his time as Minister for Health. The London Transport executive made an agreement with the Barbadian Immigration Liaison Service. Other employers, such as the British Hotel and Restaurant Association, made similar agreements. In the 1950s most Indian migrant workers to arrive in Britain were Sikhs from the rural areas of the Punjab, where the partition of the Punjab between India and Pakistan had created immense pressure on land resources during the 1950s and 1960s, greatly increasing such emigration from then on.

Whatever the specific situation within the economies of the main Commonwealth countries which led different groups of workers to migrate to Britain during the 1950s and 1960s, the overall explanation for all labour migration from the Indian sub-continent, as well as from the Caribbean, was the same—the poverty and unemployment which were a direct result of economic problems caused by years of British colonial exploitation.

Most of the first newcomers to Britain in the 1950s and 1960s tended to settle in areas of low unemployment. Therefore they inevitably gravitated towards major cities, to London in particular, but also to the Midlands and to areas further north, like Bradford. Contrary to 'popular' and racist mythology, many of the Caribbean workers who came to Britain in the 1950s and 1960s were highly skilled workers, but once here racism ensured that virtually all were forced into semi-skilled or unskilled work—often in those areas which had been partially deserted by the indigenous workforce in favour of the higher pay and better conditions in industries associated with new technology.

With discrimination widespread, nearly all black workers remained in the manual working class with little hope of promotion or mobility. Moreover, when the economy did begin to slow down in the late 1960s, it was black workers who invariably lost their jobs first. In a period of only 12 weeks during 1956, for instance, unemployment rose from 23 to 400 in Smethwick, the West Midlands town which would later become famous for the notoriously racist election campaign which the Tory candidate ran there in the early 1960s.[34] Of those who remained in work, Commonwealth migrants usually did twice the amount of shift work as other workers and on average earned significantly lower wages.

One clear indication that the overwhelming majority of migrants from the Caribbean and Indian sub-continent intended to stay in Britain for only a short period of time is this readiness on the part of most of them to migrate internally within Britain. New Commonwealth migrants were predominantly young people in their late teens or early twenties and, in the case of Caribbean migration, almost half of those who came to Britain as wage labourers in their own right were single women. Conversely most migrants from the Indian sub-continent were single or married men. Nearly all members of both groups nevertheless came to Britain with the intention of staying only temporarily, long enough to earn enough money to improve the situation back home once he or she returned to his or her family. Where fares had not been loaned directly by employers to prospective migrants, workers' fares to Britain were often paid by pooling family resources.

As the demand for labour continued to drop during the 1960s most of these temporary migrants were gradually transformed into permanent settlers, even if many still maintained a belief that they would eventually return 'home'. As unemployment began rising slowly in the 1960s and then more quickly during the 1970s, migrant workers found themselves suffering the effects disproportionately. Enticed here by bosses facing desperate labour shortages in the 1950s, most of these workers now found themselves thrown onto the scrap heap first, and re-employed last, as capitalism became less and less able to employ its workforce. The squeeze in the job market which began in the 1960s and accelerated during the 1970s was the main reason why so many New Commonwealth immigrants were forced to revise their original plans for a speedy return home, although few could have foreseen that the British economy was entering into a period of profound economic crisis from which it is yet to recover.

The Commonwealth Immigrants Act (1962)

What fundamentally transformed this situation, as well as dramatically increasing the numbers of Commonwealth migrants who did attempt to reach Britain during the early 1960s, was the Commonwealth Immigrants Bill of 1962. In the period immediately before and after the Tories introduced the 1962 Act, the entry of dependants into Britain increased almost threefold as families were left with little choice but to attempt to 'beat the act', amidst widespread fears that Britain planned to permanently close its doors to its citizens in the New Commonwealth, including the families of those already living in Britain. Total New Commonwealth immigration thus grew from 21,550 entrants in 1959, to 58,300 in 1960. A year later this last figure had more than doubled and a record 125,400 New Commonwealth immigrants entered the UK in 1961.[35] Thus the racism of Britain's Tory government led them to destroy in one single act the almost perfect symmetry which had previously existed between levels of migration into Britain and the level of demand for labour there. And if this were not irony enough, the Tory government then drew back at the last minute from restricting the right of family reunification to Commonwealth citizens under the terms of the 1962 Act and thereby scored not one but two own goals.

Even so, the Commonwealth Immigrants Bill proved to be a landmark in a much more enduring sense, with far graver consequences for future migrant workers. It was the first legislation to introduce state regulation of Commonwealth immigration and introduced the first ever entry restrictions on British Commonwealth citizens, by making primary immigration dependent upon the possession of a work voucher. Given that the intended targets of the Act were all black or Asian (and few ever even attempted to deny this), the 1962 Act also marks the first of a series of racially discriminatory pieces of legislation which have combined to lay the basis for the notoriously racist immigration laws for which Britain is so famous today. The 1962 Act enshrined in law for the first time the completely false, yet no less insidious, notion that immigration equals black immigration, a notion upon which all successive immigration legislation has been built.

In 1968, for instance, the Labour government introduced into law the nonsense of the 'New Commonwealth' which, translated, means 'black' and therefore 'unwelcome'. Not satisfied, in 1971 the Tories introduced into law the equally absurd notion of 'patriality' which, when translated, means 'white' and, by implication, 'welcome'. Overall the 1962 Act succeeded in making respectable, as well as enshrining in law, what was previously only claimed openly by isolated bigots like Enoch Powell or what was whispered in private in cabinet committees: that black immigration into Britain is a fundamentally bad thing, and that it should be prevented at all costs, except, of course, where the system would literally cease to function without it.

The politics of racism

Throughout the 1950s labour shortage was still seen as the main problem for British industries most vulnerable to the 'stop-go' cycle, like the car industry. In 1956 the *Wolverhampton Express and Star* concluded the following: 'If Britain's present boom is to be maintained, more workers must be found. Where? The new recruits to British industry must come it would seem, from abroad, from the colonies, Eire and the Continent.' So in the 1950s the Tory cabinet voted by big majorities against immigration controls. But some backbench Tories were beginning to feel confident enough to make open references in parliament to the supposed links between Commonwealth immigrants and disease, and between blacks and violent crime (despite the fact that blacks and Asians were themselves far more likely to be physically attacked than any other social group in Britain). Constant references to high birth rates amongst blacks were also made, as well as the inference that blacks in Britain were quite happy to remain unemployed, thereby implying that immigrants came to Britain only to 'scrounge' from the welfare state. These Tory back benchers were central to creating the essentially artificial link between 'race relations' and immigration which was developed during the late 1950s and early 1960s in Britain and by which British politics were 'racialised' during that period. In so doing, however, they built upon the findings of a cabinet committee, set up by Labour as far back as 1951, which recommended that any future immigration controls would 'as a general rule, be more or less confined to coloured persons'.[36]

By 1964 virtually no MP in the Commons would speak out openly in favour of unrestricted immigration and by the mid-to late 1960s levels of immigration from the Commonwealth were down to virtually zero as a direct result of government legislation. So what had changed? Mainly the state of the British economy, which by 1961 was characterised by declining economic performance. Newly arrived black and Asian workers from the Commonwealth proved to be the perfect scapegoats for the ever deepening economic troubles which the Tories now faced. Moreover, as the general election loomed nearer and nearer, their political bankruptcy became ever more visible and most were desperate to rustle up a few cheap votes in any way possible. The Tory party quickly capitulated to pressure from the right by introducing the 1962 Act.

Initially, at least, the act made little difference to real levels of Commonwealth immigration—the right of entry for dependants was not withdrawn and many continued to enter until 1967, free of control. Crucially, though, the entry of all other Commonwealth immigrants was now controlled by the state via the issuing of vouchers. Those still able to enter now had to fit into one of three categories, designed to match workers to specific jobs for which they had already been employed, or to encourage workers with very specific skills, namely those which were still in demand in the British economy, to continue to come to work in Britain. British bosses had been noticeably absent from the calls for controls and it is significant that the act in no way prevented them from recruiting that labour which was still needed.

The major difference, for the employers at least, was that the recruitment of Commonwealth labour was now conducted via the state, although this increased level of state control did not lead to the state assuming responsibility for providing housing or other services for the 40,000 or so New Commonwealth migrants who arrived each year between 1962 and 1965. The main effect of Britain's first overtly racist immigration act was thus to institutionalise racism within the machinery of the state, rather than to prevent the recruitment of necessary labour power. Black immigration was now perceived to be a problem in society at large, even though blacks, when they were needed, could still be brought to work in Britain. When the need for their labour was not so great, a thoroughly racist system of immigration controls would, moreover, help to ensure that black workers already in Britain could be blamed more easily for the rapidly growing difficulties which the economy faced in the years which immediately followed the introduction of the 1962 Act.

Labour and immigration controls

During the late 1950s the official position of the Labour Party towards immigration controls was apparently still one of principled opposition to *any* controls. Labour certainly kept quiet about this position during the 1959 election, but gave no indication that its policies towards immigration had changed in any way.[37] Even so this did not prevent the right wing of the Labour Party from making all the running over the question of immigration during the late 1950s and early 1960s. Labour MPs joined in with Tory claims that 11,000 to 12,000 immigrants were 'pouring' into Britain every year, whilst some even wrote leader articles for daily newspapers arguing the case for immigration controls. Indeed, one or two Labour MPs called in parliament for even tighter controls than those proposed by the Tories' 1962 Act.[38] Yet as late as the committee stage of the 1962 Bill Denis Healey, on behalf of the front bench of the Labour opposition, was still prepared to tell a mass meeting of Commonwealth Immigrant Organisations in Britain that a Labour government would repeal the Tories' Act.[39]

By the end of 1962, though, Harold Wilson was assuring parliament that Labour no longer contested the need for immigration controls, whilst increasing numbers of Labour MPs supported the claim that Britain could not afford to be the 'welfare state for the whole of the Commonwealth'.[40] By the time of the 1964 election the Labour Party was even more willing than the Tories to use the question of immigration controls to win votes. During the 1964 election campaign nearly twice as many Labour candidates as Tory mentioned immigration in their election addresses—and almost all of those who did made it plain that Labour was keen to continue Tory immigration policies.[41] One Labour candidate, in the Wandsworth Central seat, even issued a leaflet entitled 'Things About Immigration the Tories Want You to Forget', which stated the following:

Large-scale immigration has occurred only under this Tory government. The Tory Immigration Act has failed to control it—immigrants of all colours and races continue to arrive here.[42]

Labour's election manifesto also made it clear that Labour would retain immigration controls in all circumstances, whilst negotiating with Commonwealth countries over ways of preventing immigration 'at source'. The main explanation for Labour's *volte-face* over the question of controls is simply that it feared losing votes if it failed to take a 'tough' line on immigration. Of course, this was never openly admitted. In fact, Labour never once attempted to give any explanation for its complete turnaround over the question of controls. Roy Hattersley came the closest to an explanation during a parliamentary debate in 1965, during which he publicly bemoaned Labour's failure to support the introduction of the 1962 Act, whilst calling for a test 'to analyse which immigrants...are most likely to assimilate in our national life'.[43] In other words, the key to understanding why Labour did a complete somersault over the question of immigration controls is that it was prepared, then as now, to pander to racist ideas about immigrants in order to win votes at a general election. In the process, by failing to challenge the racism at the heart of all immigration controls—that migrant workers do not 'fit in', or are 'different', even 'inferior' in some way—the Labour Party gave significant credibility to the increasing calls for controls which both preceded and followed the introduction of the 1962 Act. That Labour reversed its earlier policy of opposing immigration controls purely for reason of electoral expediency was admitted years later by Richard Crossman in his diaries:

Ever since the Smethwick election it has been quite clear that immigration can be the greatest potential vote-loser for the Labour Party... If we are seen to be permitting a flood of immigrants to come in and blight the central areas of our cities.

Hattersley's speech is important for another reason, as it illustrates more than just the unprincipled vote gathering in which the Labour Party was prepared to indulge. The stress on 'our national life' as being somehow in need of protection also indicates very clearly Labour's emphatic belief in 'the nation', its belief in the idea that British workers and employers all have something in common by virtue of being born under the Union Jack. Any such commitment to this sort of nationalism is inevitably accompanied by an equally great commitment to the British state, including its vast machinery of racist immigration officers and controls—and this is a commitment which Labour governments both before and after the 1964 election have never flinched from making.

Even if it is true that the majority of Labour MPs are not motivated by the same kind of crude racism and bigotry which characterises the Tory party, the net result of Labour's belief in the 'national interest'—and in everything which accompanies it, including racist immigration controls—is exactly the same.

Of course, Labour attempted to complete its about turn on immigration during the early 1960s by attempting to hide behind an argument first mooted by the right wing of the Tory party, namely, that immigration controls are needed to preserve good 'race relations' in Britain. This completely insidious notion—that racism in Britain is best eradicated by inviting immigration officers to practise it at the point of entry into Britain—is best summed up by this syllogism from Roy Hattersley in 1965: 'Without integration, limitation in inexcusable: without limitation, integration is impossible.' Although the logic of this argument is quite perverse, in that it implies that black people—and not racism—should be removed from British society, it has nevertheless guided the Labour Party's basic approach to the question of immigration controls ever since, encapsulated in its recurrent theme of 'firm but fair' immigration controls.

Neither is it true, as is frequently argued by those who support immigration controls, that the implementation of controls serves to placate or silence the most racist elements in society. Indeed, the absolute opposite is true: the enactment of controls merely serves to legitimise the notion that immigrants are to blame in some way for the problems which workers face in capitalist society. Institutionalised racism, in the form of state sponsored immigration controls, is central to other forms of racism in Britain today, and even the most cursory glance at the history of immigration controls in Britain—or elsewhere in Western Europe—illustrates the point only too well. Far from placating the racists, greater controls simply serve to boost their confidence to call for even more.

This was certainly the case after the introduction of the 1962 Commonwealth Immigrants Act. The implementation of Britain's first overtly racist controls, combined with the dropping of any opposition by the Labour Party, gave a huge boost to the previously marginalised hard core of racist Tory MPs who had been most vociferous in calling for controls before 1962. Their calls for even more controls now began to take the centre stage of British politics, amidst increasing claims that the 1962 act was being evaded. When the Tories lost the 1964 election to Labour, many more Tory MPs began to raise the immigration issue.[44] As the pressure on the new Labour government grew from the right, it sadly—but predictably—surrendered to each and every new call for tighter restrictions on Commonwealth immigration, and proceeded to enact some of the most vicious controls in the history of British immigration laws.

In 1964 figures for Commonwealth immigration showed a small increase had taken place, from 66,000 in the previous year, to 75,495, an increase which was largely accounted for by women and children entering the UK to join male relatives already here, amidst continued fears that the entry of dependants would soon be prohibited.[45] These figures were leapt upon by some of right wing Tory MPs as proof that a voucher system would not by itself sufficiently reduce Commonwealth immigration into Britain.

The speed with which Labour rushed to respond to these calls for further controls was grotesque and the severity of the White Paper which the Labour government introduced in 1965 shocked even those who called most loudly for controls. Labour proceeded to reduce the number of vouchers issued each year to prospective Commonwealth migrants to only 5,000 and, in the most overtly racist move yet, removed the right of entry from British passport holders whose parents or grandparents were born outside Britain.[46] Yet this was still not enough to appease the racists, who grew ever more confident in the face of Labour's craven desire to please them. Even after the number of Commonwealth immigrants able to gain entry into Britain had started to drop dramatically—to the extent that in 1967 far less than the paltry figure of 5,000 even managed to gain access to Britain, with only 3,807 able to gain entry in that year—Powell and others instead began to call openly for repatriation. They had some success in ensuring that attention was now increasingly focused on the black population already here, and on the alleged links between blacks and violent crime and with every other social ill imaginable.

In February 1968 Enoch Powell attacked Kenyan Asians who held British passports and who therefore had the automatic right of entry into Britain. In less than three weeks Labour had responded by rushing through parliament a new immigration bill aimed at removing that right unless British passport holders had a close connection with Britain. In one single move Labour rendered 150,000 Kenyan Asians effectively 'stateless', whilst retaining a clause for those whose grandparents were born here (ie those who were white) to continue to enjoy free entry to the UK. Far from silencing the likes of Powell, Labour's abject capitulation merely encouraged him. Within weeks of Labour rushing through its new act, Powell made his most inflammatory speech yet, predicting that 'rivers of blood' would flow if immigration was not curbed further.[47] When the Labour government finally fell in 1970, its supporters demoralised and disillusioned, it left behind a legacy of racism more shameful than perhaps any other in its history.

Despite Labour's fairly transparent posturing in opposition, and its protests against the Tories' 1971 Immigration Act, little changed when it next took office. When Labour won the 1974 election it moved very quickly to tighten the rules even further.[48] It was under Labour, for instance, that gynaecological examinations of women were carried out at airports supposedly to determine their virginity, and it was during the 1974-79 Labour government that hazardous X-rays were taken at airports to determine the age of prospective entrants into Britain.[49] Within two years of winning the election Labour also joined the racist agitation which surrounded the expulsion of a small number of Asians from Malawi, evidenced by Bob Mellish's claim in 1974 that people 'cannot come here just because they have a British passport—full stop'. By now this was abundantly clear for all to see, for removing the right of British passport holders to enter the UK had, after all, been the main point of the 1968 Commonwealth Immigrants Act, which Bob Mellish's own party had forced through the Commons with obscene haste.

In reality, the episode surrounding the expulsion of the Malawi Asians in 1974 was one of the clearest examples yet of the way in which racist agitation for immigration controls has virtually nothing at all to do with the actual numbers of immigrants who attempt to gain entry to Britain at any one time. Only 250 Malawi Asians were being expelled from Malawi and all could easily have been incorporated into the voucher system for that year. Even so right wing Tory MPs tabled motions demanding urgent discussion on the 'changing demographic character of Great Britain',[50] (meaning of course the colour of people's skin) and Labour's home secretary, Roy Jenkins, responded by assuring them that Labour would maintain 'strict immigration control' and would 'root out' illegal immigrants and overstayers.[51] By 1978 Labour had buried its conscience for good, a fact demonstrated by Merlin Rees's famous television admission that all immigration controls were aimed at stopping 'coloured' immigration.[52] Of course Labour had always accepted this basic premise, which had been recommended by its own cabinet committees during the 1950s and which was institutionalised for the first time in the 1962 Act. The only difference now was that they were prepared to openly admit it.

Even so Labour's new found 'honesty' did nothing to win it the 1979 general election. Under the Labour government of 1974-1979 workers' living standards fell for the first time in real terms since the 1930s, with the working class militancy of the early 1970s held back by the Social Contract agreed between the trade union leaders and the Labour government. Against a background of deepening economic crisis unemployment rose from 500,000 to over 1.5 million while inflation ate away at the wages of those still in work. Health, education and welfare services were all cut savagely. With hopes in Labour dashed and working class confidence eroded by the policies of the TUC, a renewed racist offensive took place across British society, witnessed by the success of Nazi National Front candidates in the council elections of 1976, as well as by a sharp increase in racist murders. Although a large and vibrant anti-racist movement emerged within the working class in response to the rise of the National Front, a movement which ultimately drove the Nazis from the streets, Labour continued to move rightwards until it lost power in 1979.

Labour's final contribution to the tightening of immigration controls in Britain was its Green Paper on nationality law, which included several proposals later incorporated by Thatcher's Tory government in its 1981 Nationality Act. In 1979 Labour was thrown from office, its own culpability in creating the conditions from which the far right had been able to emerge partly concealed by widespread concern over the activities of the Nazis on the streets, as well as by the sharp move to the right within the Tory party during the late 1970s.

Racism and immigration since 1979

Under Thatcher the Tory party began moving sharply to the right over most economic and social issues well before the 1979 election. Thatcher's determination to keep the race/immigration theme at the very centre of political debate was only one part of this. As early as March 1977 Thatcher was asked to comment on the call for a complete ban on all further immigration by a Conservative candidate in a by-election, to which she replied that people's 'fears' could be ended only 'by holding out a clear prospect of an end to immigration'.[53] In April 1978 the Tory party announced its intention to introduce a new nationality law, as well as new restrictions on the entry of dependants, husbands and fiances. They also promised to create a 'register' of dependants specifically from the Indian sub-continent. In the months immediately preceding the election Thatcher repeated her earlier claim that 'British people's fears' about 'being swamped' were legitimate.[54] Nearly all of the Tory party's manifesto pledges to further tighten up Britain's system of immigration controls, which by now already ensured that New Commonwealth migration consisted only of the dependants of men who had entered Britain as migrant workers more than a decade earlier, were implemented with great speed.

New immigration rules were passed in December 1979, which further restricted the entry of Commonwealth dependants into Britain and in January 1981 the Tories passed a new Nationality Act which effectively removed the right to British citizenship from significant numbers of New Commonwealth citizens who had previously been classed as British citizens. Although Labour in opposition returned to an apparently principled position, even claiming that its own Commonwealth Immigrants Act of 1968 had been a mistake, and promising to repeal the new British Nationality Act if elected again, few people, by this time, were listening.

The Tories' new proposals were introduced into parliament amidst claims by Tory MPs, most notably Tony Marlow, that racism amongst British people was a 'natural' instinct. Marlow claimed the following in early 1980:

People have criticised these measures because they say they are racialist, as if racialist is a word of abuse. What does racialist mean? It means tribal. After all, man is a tribal animal. We have a feeling of kith and kin for people like ourselves, with our own background and culture.[55]

With mainstream Tory MPs now confident enough to be openly racist within parliament, it is hardly surprising that the far right of the Tory party grew ever more confident during the first term of Thatcher's government. Groups like the Monday Club were reactivated by MPs such as Enoch Powell and Harvey Proctor and the club's Immigration and Repatriation Policy Committee consistently put forward serious proposals during the early 1980s for the forced repatriation of 100,000 New Commonwealth immigrants each year from Britain.

This shift to the right was also evident in 'academic' circles during the early 1980s with new journals like the *Salisbury Review* regularly supporting the calls for forced repatriation as well as endorsing the claims frequently made by Tory MPs that blacks living in Britain were linked to 'vastly disproportionate' amounts of violent crime.[56] The racist image of the West Indian mugger was now accompanied by that of the 'wily Asian' in the right wing press, amidst claims from Tory MPs that Indian and Pakistani immigrants were abusing the arranged marriage system and evading the new immigration rules in order to gain access to the British 'honeypot'. During Thatcher's first year of office a huge increase in raids carried out by police and immigration officers took place, mainly on Asian businesses with large numbers of workers, the vast majority of whom had committed no offence yet who were questioned and arrested under the new immigration legislation. Warrants were now issued without having to refer to the names of particular individuals. These effectively gave carte blanche to police and immigration officials to raid both the businesses and the homes of black and Asian residents in Britain. It created a situation where most Asians and West Indians in Britain faced little choice but to carry their passport around with them at all times.

Thatcher's regime also saw Britain acquiring one of the worst records in Europe in its treatment of asylum seekers, the only significant group of immigrants now able to gain access, however temporarily, to the UK. Between 1984 and 1986 British immigration officers accepted for asylum only 240 for every 1 million of the UK's inhabitants, ie a proportion of 0.024 percent as compared with nearly 5,000 per 1 million

inhabitants for Sweden and more than 4,000 for Denmark and
Switzerland. In 1981 more than 60 percent of asylum seekers who
managed to enter Britain were eventually granted refugee status but by
1988 the figure had dropped to only 25 percent. Even this dramatic
reduction is worse than it seems, for the total number of asylum seekers
who managed to even reach Britain to claim asylum in the first place was
reduced significantly by Thatcher's introduction of stiff fines in 1987
against airlines and shipping companies which carried passengers
without proper documentation or visas.[57] This ensured that a significant
drop took place in the numbers of potential refugees able to leave their
country of origin in the first place, since most refugees are forced to flee
persecution using forged or inadequate documentation, without which
escape would be simply impossible. The idea that potential refugees
could simply queue at British embassies abroad to apply for the required
entry visa for Britain was always a nonsense—but it is still enshrined
within British asylum law. By forcing airline and shipping companies to
act as immigration officials, or face huge fines of thousands of pounds
for each 'illegal' asylum seeker on board, Thatcher ensured that most
would simply refuse to take on board any individual whose real identity
was in doubt.

Desperately seeking asylum: the 1993 Asylum and Immigration Appeals Act

After the Tories' doubled the 'carriers' liability' fine in 1991, the total
number of asylum applicants to arrive in Britain was virtually halved by
the end of the 1992.[58] Literally thousands of refugees were prevented
from fleeing persecution or death as a result of this legislation, simply
because they were unable to persuade airline or shipping companies to
allow them to board without a full set of travel documents.

The other main method by which the British government prevents
refugees or other migrants from leaving their country of origin is through
the imposition of visa restriction. By 1991 residents of more than 90
countries were subject to visa restrictions on travel to the UK. The
response of John Major's government to the growing number of people
displaced by civil wars across the world during the 1990s was simply to
add even more countries to the list. In 1992 visa restrictions were
imposed on the former Yugoslavia, making it impossible for most
victims of the war to leave, whilst in early 1995 victims of the civil war
in Sierra Leone were prevented from coming to Britain by the imposition
of visa restrictions. The barbaric reality of the plight which Britain and
other Western European states have created for refugees and other
migrants was brought home chillingly in late 1992, when a group of

eight Ghanaian stowaways were thrown overboard by the crew of a German ship, worried that the carriers' liability fine would be deducted from their wages. Only one of the group, Kingsley Ofusu, survived to tell the tale. Although many other similar incidents were reported during the 1980s and 1990s, many more are never reported, simply because none of the stowaways survive their journey. Those who do survive face a fate which is little better—such as the one remaining member of a group of Romanian asylum seekers who travelled to Britain in early 1994 in a ship's container which was also carrying toxic waste which led to the deaths of his companions. Within months of finally arriving in the UK he was summarily refused asylum, and forcibly returned to Romania by the British authorities. Not surprisingly, then, forced deportations—using all the paraphernalia which led to the killing of Joy Gardner—are at record levels under the Tories, particularly since the introduction of the Asylum and Immigration Appeals Act in 1993.

Under the provisions of the 1993 Act huge numbers of asylum seekers are now deported from Britain within only days of arrival, without having had their asylum application even considered here. This is 'justified' by the fact that their ship or aeroplane stopped in a third country on its way to Britain and that this supposedly gave any 'genuine' refugee the opportunity to claim asylum there instead. Throughout 1993 and 1994 many potential refugees were thus bounced around between various West European states, most of which were as unwilling as Britain to consider asylum application sympathetically once a prospective asylum seeker had been dumped unceremoniously in their territory by the British authorities. Ever since the introduction of these new procedures in 1993 large numbers of these refugees have been forcibly deported back to their country of origin by these so called 'safe' third countries. Amnesty International has confirmed in some cases that the asylum seeker has been murdered by that country's authorities soon after involuntarily arriving back home.

For those lucky enough to have their asylum applications considered in Britain, by virtue of the fact that their plane did not touch down anywhere before it arrived in the UK, huge numbers of potential refugees are now detained from the moment they arrive in Britain, despite having committed no crime whatsoever other than having fled persecution and possible death in their homelands. In 1993 the detention of asylum seekers more than doubled in Britain. Some 10,530 people were detained in that year alone, under immigration detention powers.[59] Some were held in high security prisons as well as in brand new purpose built immigration detention centres like that at Campsfield House in Kidlington, Oxford. Appalling conditions and the brutal treatment of asylum seekers at these centres were brought to light in early 1994 by a wave of hunger strikes by prisoners, which helped to initiate sizeable pickets in support of the hunger strikers.

Fortress Europe

Successive British governments have undoubtedly led the way in introducing these hideous new methods for preventing the entry of refugees into Britain, but Europe has been quick to follow. In December 1993 the European Commission proposed sweeping new immigration restrictions, which will bring Fortress Europe more than a few steps closer. The commission drew up a list of 128 countries whose nationals will require visas before crossing over Europe's borders, the vast majority of which are Asian and African countries. The commission also allowed individual member states to impose further restrictions on individuals from other countries not included on the list, and most Western European countries have already indicated their great enthusiasm for joining Britain in its brutal treatment of asylum seekers. Wim Kwok, the deputy prime minister of the Netherlands, declared as early as 1991 that anyone rejected for asylum should be deported 'without delay', while Edith Cresson, the French prime minister during 1991, recommended 'special flights' from France for unsuccessful asylum seekers, to act as a deterrent to anyone else planning to make the same mistake they had.[60]

After decades of shedding crocodile tears for the populations of Eastern Europe, the ruling classes of Western Europe are now erecting their own iron curtain to keep a potential immigrant population out of Western Europe, a population which most states estimate will still amount to less than 1 percent of the EC population over the next five years, and this against an estimated decline in the birth rate in many of these member states over the next ten years. The enthusiasm with which the EC states have attempted to formulate a 'common' immigration policy has been tempered only by their complete inability to agree upon exactly which coasts and frontiers should be policed by the new draconian European immigration controls. All this is in spite of the fact that Europe receives only about 5 percent of the world's estimated 17.5 million refugees. More than 80 percent of refugees in the world today are concentrated in the poorest countries of the world.

The current tightening of asylum procedures in the West was preceded by the virtual ending of all other forms of immigration in many advanced capitalist countries by the mid-1970s. At the start of the 1970s there were between 9 and 11.5 million migrant workers in Western Europe as well as sizeable numbers who had been forced to enter the West illegally. By 1974 all the labour importing countries had slammed their doors to prospective migrants from outside Western Europe[61] and by 1977 more than 1 million temporary workers had been expelled from various countries across Western Europe. The overriding reason for this dramatic turnabout lies in the ending of the long post-war boom and the return of crisis to the system during the late 1960s. This process has continued largely uninterrupted until the present day and has effectively brought to an end the need for migrant labour in those economies. As boom turned to crisis in the late 1960s and early 1970s overall profit rates across the business and manufacturing sectors of the advanced capitalist countries fell by one fifth, and although patterns of capital accumulation tended to maintain a relatively high demand for labour as late as the early 1970s the rate of growth in the total number of people at work still proceeded more slowly than the overall rate of capital accumulation.

This is partly because new means of production introduced during the boom years frequently embodied higher and higher degrees of mechanisation which increased the rate of exploitation of individual workers but which tended to reduce in the long term the number of workers actually employed.[62] During most of the boom years the non-agricultural labour force did continue to grow by an average of 1.7 percent each year in most of the advanced capitalist countries, but with immigrant labour an increasingly less important part of that process as time went on. Between 1968 and 1973, for instance, immigration accounted for only 0.1 percent of the overall growth in the labour force of most of the leading capitalist countries.[63] The greatest part of the increase was accounted for by the increased participation of women workers in full time employment as well as by workers moving into industry from the shrinking agricultural labour force.[64] Even during the brief upswing in the world economy between 1972 and 1973, when a quite serious mismatch of skills and labour demand did emerge, the recovery was too short lived to create the need for large scale immigration to meet this demand.

After 1973 a deep crisis of profitability returned to the system, and production during the next decade grew at less than half the rate of the 1960s with a further slowing down evident from 1979 onwards.[65] After 1973 the spectre of mass unemployment returned to haunt the system and by 1975 unemployment in the OECD countries was already up to 15 million. By 1983 that figure had more than doubled to 32 million with at least one in three of the new jobs created in Europe after this time filled by members of the registered unemployed.[66]

With the exception of a few very short lived periods of recovery the global economy has remained in a deep crisis since the early 1970s with serious labour shortages, in the West at least, apparently a thing of the past. With capitalism no longer heavily reliant upon migrant labour as it was during the long post-war boom, both Tory and Labour governments throughout the advanced capitalist world have rushed to erect the most rigid and restrictive machinery of immigration controls in the history of capitalism, not only to keep out those migrant workers on whose labour the system depended a few decades ago, but also as a means of dividing, and therefore controlling, the working class already living within the borders of their respective nation states.

Internal controls

Immigration controls are not designed purely to keep out migrant workers and refugees from the territory of a particular state. They are also a powerful weapon with which the ruling class in modern capitalist society attempts to divide workers by stoking up racism *within* national boundaries. Immigration controls are the sharp end of institutionalised racism in most Western European states today—racism directed not only at prospective migrants, but as much at black or 'foreign' workers already living within its borders.

Thus the history of immigration controls in Britain is also the history of concerted attempts, by Tory politicians and the tabloid press, to fan the flames of racism within British society. Every new set of immigration controls, from the 1905 Aliens Act to the Tories' new legislation planned for autumn 1995, has always been accompanied by claims that immigrant workers in Britain are to blame for unemployment, poor housing, and street crime—for all the problems which workers experience in capitalist society on a daily basis. Instead of workers blaming government policies or capitalism itself for the inability of the system to meet even their most basic needs, successive Tory governments and their friends in the gutter press use the question of immigration, and the calls for tighter controls, in an attempt to divert discontent away from the real source of the problems and towards immigrants instead.

In Britain today the focus for racism has centred around two 'types' of migrants: so called 'bogus' refugees and 'illegal' immigrants. During the period immediately preceding the introduction of the 1993 Act, Tories such as Kenneth Clarke repeatedly claimed that nine out of ten claims for refugee status were 'bogus' or 'unfounded', a statement which went completely unchallenged by Labour. Indeed, Roy Hattersley went even further during a parliamentary debate in 1991, when he assured the Commons that Labour too would weed out the 'undeserving':

Let us make clear—beyond doubt I hope—that bogus asylum seekers must be prevented from entering the country. This is an honourable and sensible objective and our amendment reflects our determination to ensure that bogus asylum seekers are identified and denied entry.[67]

Far from Labour holding an 'honourable' position on the question of refugees, Hattersley's statement, echoed by Blair when he was shadow spokesman for home affairs, illustrates Labour's complete acquiescence to the Tories over the need for tough, racist immigration controls in Britain. Labour's abject failure to challenge one of the main pretexts for further tightening controls, namely that most asylum seekers are 'bogus', also signals the extent to which Labour has been prepared to collude with the racism at the heart of all immigration controls. There is, of course, nothing 'bogus' about the vast majority of claims for political asylum in the United Kingdom. The Tories' figure of 'more than 80 percent' is drawn purely from the number of refugee claims which its Home Office ministers now reject—as if that were a real test of the 'genuine' nature of claims!

The real implications of the Tories' claims, that most refugees are 'bogus', was further underlined in the early 1990s when Kenneth Baker, then home secretary, was found in contempt of court for forcibly returning a asylum seeker to Zaire—who was then murdered by the same authorities whom he had fled to Britain to escape. Labour's refusal to challenge the Tories' pernicious claims about 'bogus' refugees has not only meant that the Tories' aim (of deporting as many refugees and immigrants as it possibly can in as short a time as possible) has been more easily realised over the last few years. It has also given credence and respectability to the racist notion that immigrants come to Britain to 'scrounge' off the welfare state, at the expense of 'British' workers. After all, the Tories' attacks on 'bogus' refugees are as much about whipping up racism against immigrants already living in Britain as they are about attempting to justify the record number of asylum seekers whom Britain now turns away.

This is equally true of the hysteria which Tory MPs have recently tried to whip up over so called 'illegal immigrants' living in Britain following the resignation of Home Office minister Charles Wardle in early 1995, amidst claims that Britain's surrender of its passport controls within the European Union would lead to a huge influx of immigrants. The cabinet rushed to placate the right wing 'Eurosceptics' inside the party.[68] Within weeks of Wardle's resignation the government had forced through legislation to create its aptly named 'White List' of countries from which asylum claims will no longer be entertained, and announced a new 'crackdown' on 'illegal' immigrants. Yet is now so hard to get into Britain, that even the bosses' favourite magazine, the *Economist*, is unable to understand why the Tories should be planning further legislation:

[The Tory party's] *policy has already reduced the inflow to a trickle. The number of successful applications for British citizenship* [is] *at its lowest for ten years. Nowhere in Britain is being swamped.* [69]

In fact, the planned legislation has far less to do with tightening up external controls (although stricter visa requirements and the removal of the right of appeal in some asylum cases will certainly achieve this) than it has to do with pointing the finger at every non-white worker in Britain. Even by the Tory party's own admission, the latest 'crackdown' by Howard is an attempt to put 'clear blue water' between themselves and Labour.[70] In other words, the planned new laws, and the hysterical claims surrounding them, are nothing but a crude attempt to play the 'race card' in the run up to the next general election. By witch hunting and scare-mongering over the relatively tiny number of illegal immigrants who are estimated to live in Britain, the most unpopular government this century hopes to divert anger and attention away from itself and towards black or 'foreign' workers instead.

If the Tories succeed in pushing this legislation through, every non-white worker in Britain will be targeted as a potentially 'illegal' immigrant. Under the proposed plans, the Tories vitually intend to turn doctors, teachers, DSS officers and local government workers into immigration officers. By law, all these different groups of workers will be obliged to check the immigration status of anybody whom they 'suspect' of being an illegal immigrant with the Home Office before providing the required service, be it urgent medical care, income support, or schooling for a child. In other words, the Tories are attempting to institutionalise racist policies and practices within every school, hospital, DSS and council office in Britain. The onus will be on individual blacks or Asians to prove that they are here legally. The arrests and detentions of British-born black workers in mid-1995, after a list of 600 council employees with names of African origin was passed from Hackney council to the Home Office for 'investigation' into their immigration status, is only a small glimpse of what is possible if the Tories get away with their planned new laws. Conversely, the excellent response of workers in Hackney council, who voted to strike in response, is a clear example of the black and white working class unity which can resist the Tories' racist plans.

Equally clearly the fight against immigration controls in the future will not be able to rely on Tony Blair's 'New Labour'. When Jack Straw, Labour's shadow home secretary, told the *New Statesman* that 'you couldn't get a cigarette paper between Labour and the Tories over the question of immigration', he was speaking the truth.[71] It was, after all, Jack Straw who, alongside Michael Howard, refused to accept the 1987 Single European Act, which provides for the free movement of people within Europe—until a guarantee could be won from Europe's Council of Ministers that Europe's external borders would be tightened up further.[72] The Labour Party might have called the 1993 Asylum Act

'shabby and mean', but Labour has mounted one of the weakest oppositions imaginable to the huge tightening up of asylum and immigration
procedures which has taken place in the last two years alone.[73] Labour's
shadow spokesman on immigration, Kim Howells, has maintained a
deafening silence in the face of the record levels of deportations, detentions and even deaths which now characterise Britain's immigration
policies. Instead Labour in opposition has simply pandered to the Tories'
claims about 'bogus' refugees, desperate to convince any potentially
racist voters that Labour too will be 'tough' on immigration.

In the run up to the next election it is highly likely that the pressure on
Labour from the Tories will grow—pressure on Labour to prove it won't
be 'soft' on immigration. There is little reason to believe that Tony Blair
will be unwilling to comply. Unlike previous leaders of Labour in opposition, who promised to repeal Tory immigration laws, Tony Blair is
promising to do absolutely nothing except, ominously, what is 'best for
Britain'. Electoralism and nationalism remain at the very heart of Tony
Blair's 'New Labour'. Any strategy for fighting racist immigration controls which looks to the Labour Party leadership is therefore doomed to
failure.

Instead, effective opposition to racist immigration controls will rely, as
it has done in the past, upon the efforts of black and white workers themselves, fighting together from below against the new laws. Encouragingly,
the tightening of controls over the last number of years has been accompanied by a significant increase in the number of successful campaigns
against individual deportations. These campaigns have united black and
white workers both inside and outside the workplace. Growing numbers
of workers in Britain identify with the movement against the detention of
immigrants, witnessed by the number of trade union banners apparent at
demonstrations outside immigration detention centres in June 1995, and
by the increasing number of trade unions willing to campaign in support
of individuals facing deportation.

Black and white working class unity is also the key to fighting racism
in a wider sense. In modern capitalist society, opposition to immigration
is one of the main focuses for racism, and for racist ideas in society.
Under capitalism workers are forced to compete for the scarce economic
resources available to the working class. Racist ideas can get a hearing—
despite the fact that black or Asian workers in Britain are between three
and four times more likely to be unemployed than white workers, and
invariably live in much poorer housing. Historically Nazi organisations
have attempted to build support inside the working class by using arguments which seek to blame immigrants for workers' problems. That they
have been relatively unsuccessful in recent years, in Britain at least, testifies to the strong traditions of black and white unity which exist inside the

working class. Ultimately, though, fighting racism and fascism means fighting the system which produces the conditions for it to grow, namely capitalism. Immigration and racist immigration controls are both intrinsic parts of the capitalist system. As such, effective opposition to immigration controls ultimately means challenging the very foundations of capitalism itself.

Notes

1   C Homes, *John Bull's Island: Immigration and British Society 1871-1971* (Macmillan, 1988), p3.
2   P Fryer, *Aspects of British Black History* (Index Books, 1993), p12.
3   A L Morton, *A People's History of England* (Lawrence and Wishart, 1994), pp279-280.
4   C Holmes, op cit, pp20-22.
5   Ibid, pp14-15.
6   H Zinn, *A People's History of the United States* (Longman, 1980), ch 10.
7   C Holmes, op cit, pp14-15.
8   P Foot, *Immigration and Race in British Politics* (Penguin, 1965), p89.
9   Ibid, pp85-91.
10 L James, 'Bound for the Golden Medina', *Socialist Review* (London, issue 81), p24.
11 Ibid, p24.
12 P Foot, op cit, p89.
13 C Holmes, op cit, pp94-96.
14 P Foot, op cit, p110.
15 C Holmes, op cit, p163.
16 Ibid, p164.
17 Armstrong, Glyn and Harrison, *Capitalism since World War Two* (Fontana, 1984), p25.
18 Ibid, p69.
19 C Holmes, op cit, pp211-212.
20 For detail on Britain's treatment of European volunteer workers after the Second World War, see C Holmes, op cit, p210.
21 Ibid, p116.
22 P Foot, op cit, p116.
23 C Holmes, op cit, p214.
24 P Foot, op cit, p124.
25 T Cliff and D Gluckstein, *The Labour Party: A Marxist History* (Bookmarks, 1988), p227.
26 Ibid, p257.
27 Armstrong, Glyn and Harrison, op cit, p193.
28 R Miles and A Phizacklea, *White Man's Country* (Pluto Press, 1984), pp148-149.
29 Ibid, p150.
30 C Holmes, op cit, pp216-217.
31 P Foot, op cit, p121.
32 Ibid, p135.
33 C Holmes, op cit, pp220-221.
34 P Foot, op cit, pp13-14.
35 Ibid, p126.
36 R Miles and A Phizacklea, op cit, pp25-26.
37 P Foot, op cit, p170.

38 Ibid, pp168-169.
39 Ibid, p173.
40 Ibid, p177.
41 Ibid, p181.
42 Ibid, p181.
43 Ibid, p193.
44 R Miles and A Phizacklea, op cit, p57.
45 Ibid, p40.
46 Ibid, pp53-54.
47 Powell is quoted in T Cliff and D Gluckstein, op cit, p293.
48 R Miles and A Phizacklea, op cit, p 96.
49 Quoted in ibid, p99.
50 Ibid, p98.
51 Ibid, p100.
52 Ibid, p106.
53 Ibid, p106.
54 Ibid, p106.
55 Ibid, p108.
56 Ibid, p113.
57 *Immigration Controls are out of Control* (Greater Manchester Immgration Aid Unit, 1993), p10.
58 *Daily Telegraph*, 12 January 1993.
59 *Hansard*, 29 June 1994, Column 624.
60 *Socialist Review*, 'The New Iron Curtain' (London, issue 148).
61 R Miles and A Phizacklea, op cit, p150.
62 Ibid, p154 (see also Armstrong, Glyn and Harrison, op cit, p243).
63 Armstrong, Glyn and Harrison, op cit, p244.
64 Ibid, p244.
65 Ibid, p323.
66 Ibid, p324.
67 Greater Manchester Immigration Aid Unit, op cit, p7.
68 *Guardian*, 14 March 1995.
69 *Economist*, 18 September 1993.
70 *Times*, 24 March 1995.
71 *Guardian*, 3 March 1995.
72 *Guardian*, 24 March 1995.
73 *Guardian*, 3 November 1992.

Is Marxism deterministic?

JOHN MOLYNEUX

'Philosophers have interpreted the world in various ways, the point, however, is to change it.'

This, the most famous of all Marx quotations, written almost at the beginning of his political and theoretical development, points to the fact that from the outset Marx was driven by a passionate will to fight for a better society. Engels, speaking at Marx's graveside, testified to the fact that this passionate will survived throughout his life:

> *For Marx was before all else a revolutionist. His real mission in life was to contribute, in one way or another, to the overthrow of capitalist society and the state institutions which it had brought into being, to contribute to the liberation of the modern proletariat... Fighting was his element. And he fought with a passion, a tenacity and a success such as few could rival.*[1]

The same, of course, is true for the overwhelming majority of socialists and Marxists today. Our starting point is the desire to fight back, the wish to contribute to the making of a better world. It is this which leads us to Marxist theory, rather than Marxist theory which makes us want to change things. Perhaps somewhere there is someone who made an exhaustive study of all of Marxism and of all rival philosophical, historical, social and economic theories and on that basis, at the age of 90, decided to become a Marxist. If so I have yet to encounter them.

However, it was also Marx's great achievement that he transformed socialism from a utopia into a science, or more accurately, from a utopia or a conspiracy into a science. Prior to Marx there were two dominant approaches to the establishment of socialism. The first, exemplified by Saint-Simon and Fourier in France and Owen in Britain, was to paint such a beautiful picture of socialism as a more rational form of society than capitalism that sooner or later everyone, including the ruling class, would be persuaded of its benefits. The second, derived from the Jacobin tradition in the French Revolution, exemplified in the 19th century by Blanqui, was that a small secret conspiracy of enlightened revolutionaries should seize power by means of a coup d'état and impose socialism on society from above.

Marx rejected both these approaches, not only by espousing socialism from below, by which he meant the self emancipation of the working class, but also by insisting that such emancipation was possible only on the basis of the internal contradictions and social forces objectively at work within capitalism. In *The Communist Manifesto* he wrote:

> *The theoretical conclusions of the Communists are in no way based on ideas or principles that have been invented, or discovered, by this or that would-be universal reformer. They merely express, in general terms, actual relations springing from an existing class struggle, from a historical movement going on under our very eyes.*[2]

And in November 1850, following the defeat of the 1848 revolutions, Marx wrote:

> *In view of the general prosperity which now prevails and permits the productive forces of bourgeois society to develop as rapidly as is at all possible within the framework of bourgeois society, there can be no question of any real revolution... A new revolution will be made possible only as the result of a new crisis, but is just as certain as is the coming of the crisis itself.*[3]

Socialist theory, therefore, had to be founded on the scientific study of history and economics. Socialist strategy had to be founded on the scientific analysis of the objective situation. Revolutionary enthusiasm alone was not enough. Once again these problems are still with us. How many ardent new converts to socialism have felt they had only to tell everyone they met the good news for them all to see the light? How many young revolutionaries, after their first dramatic confrontation with the forces of the state in Trafalgar Square or Hyde Park, have thought that with a few more demonstrations like that the revolution would be round the corner?

These two elements, the revolutionary will to change the world and scientific analysis of the laws of history and society, are both present in Marx and Marxism. Individual lines of Marx can be quoted to make him appear the partisan of one element of the other. Taken in isolation, 'Philosophers have interpreted the world in various ways, the point, however, is to change it', might suggest complete indifference to philosophy or even theory as a whole. Whereas, 'The windmill gives you society with the feudal lord; the steam mill, society with the industrial capitalist',[4] might be held to suggest that new technology—the internet perhaps—will give us socialism without any revolutionary struggle or intervention. In reality, however, both activism and science coexist throughout Marx's life and work, and the history of Marxism.

But is there not an inconsistency here? If Marxism claims that history is governed by laws and human behaviour is shaped by material conditions, how can Marxism also claim that revolutionary socialist activity is vital? Or, to put it even more bluntly, if, as is sometimes claimed, Marx 'proved' that socialism is inevitable, why do we need to fight for it?

All of this raises the question of determinism—that is, the question of the extent to which history is determined by economic and other social forces independent of our will and actions as revolutionaries. It also raises the closely related question of the extent to which Marxism should be regarded as a deterministic theory.

Before dealing directly with these issues it is worth noting that bourgeois thought has never been able to resolve the problem of determinism. Rather it has swung back and forth between voluntarist idealism, which ignores social conditions and places all the emphasis on 'great' individuals and ideas, and mechanical materialism which stresses the unchangeable nature of people and society. Both these positions reflect aspects of bourgeois society viewed from the top down. On the one hand the bourgeoisie standing at the head of society, freed from productive labour and living off the exploitation of others, is able to flatter itself that its ideas and deeds rule the world. On the other hand looking down on the masses it sees them there as mere objects, passively driven this way and that by the requirements of capital accumulation. Bourgeois ideology thus attacks Marxism both for being too deterministic and for not being deterministic enough.

From Max Weber onwards bourgeois sociology and its related disciplines have condemned Marxism for its 'crude' economic determinism, its underestimation of the autonomy of ideology, politics and culture and its insistence on the central importance of class. Bourgeois historians have repeatedly tried to undermine any notion of an overall pattern of development in world history, concentrating their fire particularly on the schema outlined by Marx in *The Communist Manifesto*, and attacking the idea that the English and French Revolutions had any determinate class character or any historical necessity.

At the same time the socio-biologists have condemned Marxism and every form of left wing and socialist thought for its 'utopian' failure to grasp that inequality, hierarchy, class and competition (along with war, racism and sexism) are encoded in our genes and thus ineradicable.

Debates about determinism have also occurred amongst those claiming allegiance to Marxism. At different points in time both passive determinist and highly voluntarist interpretations of Marxism have flourished. The most important example of the determinist trend was the version of Marxism developed by Karl Kautsky which dominated German Social Democracy and the Second International in the period leading up to the First World War. In Kautsky's view the economic laws of capitalism guaranteed the growth in numbers and consciousness of the working class to the point where power would 'automatically' fall into its hands. All that was required of the socialist movement was that it build up its organisations, strengthen its vote and avoid adventures while patiently waiting for economic development to do its work.[5] It was of this period that Gramsci wrote that 'the deterministic, fatalistic and mechanistic element has been a direct ideological "armour" emanating from the philosophy of praxis [Marxism—JM] rather like religion or drugs'.[6]

At the opposite pole, the most extreme cases of voluntarism trading under a Marxist label were Maoism and Guevarism. Maoism proclaimed not only the possibility of industrialising China by will power in the disastrous Great Leap Forward but even the direct transition to complete communism in China alone without any regard for objective material circumstances (this is discussed further below). Guevarism, basing itself on the special case of Cuba, developed a theory of revolution instigated by a small band of guerillas in the countryside. 'It is not necessary', wrote Guevara, 'to wait until all the conditions for making revolution exist: the insurrection can create them'.[7]

Revolutionary Marxists have always sought to combat both these positions. Luxemburg, Lenin and Trotsky, followed later by Lukacs and Gramsci, subjected the fatalism and passive expectancy of the Second International to devastating criticism. Lenin and Trotsky also took up arms against the ultra-left voluntarist trend that developed among European communists in the early years of the Communist International.[8] In the 1950s and 1960s it was largely supporters of this journal who produced a historical materialist critique of Maoism and Castroism.[9] The problem of determinism, however, does not go away. The structure of capitalist society with its elevation of 'great' individuals and its suppression of the personality of the masses generates both mechanical determinism and voluntarist idealism and these pressures continue to bear upon Marxists.

Its is against this background that this article attempts to outline and defend an interpretation of historical materialism which avoids both these dangers remaining thoroughly materialist and resolutely activist. The first step in its argument is to consider absolute determinism and absolute indeterminism as limiting cases.

Determinism: absolute and relative

By absolute determinism I mean the view that every event in the history of the universe from the big bang to the end of time and every human action from the writing of *Capital* to whether or not I raise my right eyebrow is inevitable and could not be other than it has been, is or will be. The argument in favour of absolute determinism is that every event/action has its cause or causes, and that these causes determine precisely the nature of the said event/action and that these causes are themselves completely determined by prior causes. Thus every particular event or action is part of an infinitely complex but absolutely inevitable chain reaction inherent in the singularity or whatever lay at the origin of the universe.

Historically this position has its roots in Newtonian physics from which it draws its 'billiard-ball' view of causality (a view in which the causation of all events and processes is seen as analogous to the way in which the motion of a billiard ball is wholly determined by the speed and angle with which it is struck by another billiard ball).[10] However, it also involves the belief that human behaviour is 'ultimately' reducible to the movements of the physical particles of which humans are made up and which are held to obey universal natural laws. Some such view as this, even if not openly proclaimed, seems to have influenced those Marxists who have held an absolute determinist position. Such Marxists, however, have generously held that for the purposes of social analysis it was unnecessary to effect a reduction to the level of physics since human behaviour was governed by social laws which were akin to natural laws in their operation.

Discussing absolute determinism, Ralph Miliband comments, 'This is not a view that can be argued with: it can only be accepted or rejected. I reject it and pass on'.[11] Miliband has a point in that it is impossible to cite empirical evidence which refutes absolute determinism (just as it is impossible to cite facts which 'prove' it). Nevertheless it is a view which can be argued with. Bearing in mind Marx's dictum that:

> *In practice man must prove the truth, that is, the reality and power, the this-sidedness of his thinking. The dispute over the reality or non-reality of thinking which is isolated from practice is a pure **scholastic** question.*[12]

It is possible to assess the advantages and disadvantages of absolute determinism from the standpoint of practice.

Absolute determinism has two important merits vis-a-vis anti or indeterminist theories and for this reason has played at times a certain progressive role. First it obliges us to look for materialist explanations of events and phenomena, be they wars, revolutions, juvenile crime or child sex abuse, rather than simply ascribing them to chance, divine or satanic intervention, or personal wickedness. Second, as Gramsci notes, when the working class was going through a period of defeats, mechanical determinism could become 'a tremendous force of moral resistance, of cohesion and of patient and obstinate perseverance. I have been defeated for a moment but the tide of history is working for me in the long term'.[13] Nevertheless it has a number of disadvantages which require its rejection.

First of all absolute determinism is, in practice, impossible to live by. The fact is that all human beings experience making decisions or choices. While it is obviously true that none of these decisions can ever be completely 'free' if by 'free' is meant uninfluenced by prior conditioning and present circumstances, it is no less true that we distinguish between decisions that are strongly constrained or coerced, for example, those taken at gunpoint or under threat of starvation, and those which are voluntary or relatively so. If this distinction and the whole experience of decision making is an illusion, as the absolute determinist must claim, it is an illusion which is inescapable in practical life, including for the absolute determinist. Consequently in practice absolute determinism always contains an escape clause through which voluntarism returns by the back door. Typically it results in what Marx, in his critique of Feuerbach's mechanical materialism, described as 'dividing society into two parts, one of which is superior to the other'.[14]

Secondly, the Newtonian foundations of absolute determinism have been undermined by subsequent scientific developments such as thermodynamics, quantum mechanics including the Heisenberg Uncertainty Principle and Schrödinger's Equation, and, most recently, the rise of chaos theory.[15] For our purposes the two key points are that quantum mechanics, which deals with the behaviour of elementary particles, provides laws which are probabilistic rather than absolutely deterministic and that chaos theory shows that 'the tiniest difference in initial conditions (of a natural system such as the weather) could lead to enormous and unpredictable differences in outcome'.[16] Of course it is a crude error to generalise mechanically from natural science to social science and it is perfectly possible that aspects of human behaviour, and therefore of history, are more strictly determined than the behaviour of sub-atomic particles and the weather (just as quantum mechanics allows Newtonian laws of motion to remain valid within certain limits). Nevertheless these scientific advances challenge the widespread implicit identifications of science with absolute determinism.

Thirdly the historical experience of the working class movement has shown that absolute determinism has tended to encourage serious political errors, in particular passivity at moments of revolutionary crisis and underestimation of the role of the revolutionary party. These questions will be discussed later but quotations from Gramsci and Trotsky both make the point. Gramsci, who had bitter personal experience of the damaging effects of deterministic passivity on the part of the Italian Socialist Party in 1919-1920, comments (in the obscure language he adopted to deceive the censor):

> *But when the subaltern becomes directive...mechanism at a certain point becomes an imminent danger... The boundaries and the dominion of the 'force of circumstance' becomes restricted. But why? Because, basically, if yesterday the subaltern element was a thing, today is no longer a thing but an historical person, a protagonist...an agent, necessarily active and taking the initiative.*[17]

Trotsky, reflecting on his non-Bolshevisim prior to 1917, explained it in terms of his deterministic belief 'that the revolution would force the Mensheviks...to follow a revolutionary path', and offered this self criticism:

> *I underestimated the importance of preparatory ideological selection and of political case-hardening. On questions of the inner development of the party I was guilty of a sort of social revolutionary fatalism.*[18]

Absolute determinism therefore, must be rejected because it fails the decisive test of practice on three levels: the level of everyday life, the level of scientific practice and the level of political practice.

At the opposite pole to absolute determinism stands absolute indeterminism, the idea that human beings can do whatever they want without constraint and that everything which happens in history is purely accidental. This is such an absurd position that it is hard to see how it could be given coherent formulation. It is an inescapable fact that human behaviour is constrained and determined in a multitude of ways by, for example, the law of gravity or by the fact that if body temperature falls below a certain level we die. However strong, rather than absolute, indeterminism enjoys widespread circulation. By strong indeterminism I mean the denial of any overall shape or pattern of development in history and a heavy emphasis on the role of individuals as masters of their own fate and makers of history. In recent years postmodernism, with its 'incredulity towards metanarratives',[19] has been the dominant academic representative of this view. In this respect the postmodernists are singing an old song long intoned by bourgeois historians of various persuasions. It also underpins innumerable second rate journalistic accounts of events purely in terms of the whims and personalities of individual politicians and leaders, and finds expression in numerous popular sayings such as 'Life is what you make of it', 'If you believe in yourself everything is possible', or, 'If you want something badly enough you can get it.'

Such strong indeterminism need not detain us long. It is plainly ideological in that it serves to mask all the real social forces, the concentrations and structures of economic, political, military and ideological power, which both shape individuals and limit their freedom of action. It mitigates against any attempt to consciously make history or change society by rendering history and society unintelligible. It is also plainly false. It is not true that the mass of working class children can grow up to be brain surgeons or film stars if they try hard enough. Quite apart from factors such as early social conditioning, economic deprivation and poor education there is the simple fact that the vacancies for brain surgeons and film stars are strictly limited. Strong indeterminism is refuted by the most elementary sociological evidence such as education, crime or health statistics which, despite their numerous problems and limitations, all demonstrate beyond serious question the powerful influence of, among other things, social class on life chances and social behaviour.

Strong indeterminism is just as impossible to live by as absolute determinism. Everyday life depends on the ability to predict both natural phenomena and human actions: that it will be cold in the winter and warmer in the summer; that barley seed will grow into barley, not wheat; that the number 17 bus will go to the town centre; that if you sell your labour power to an employer you will be paid at the end of the week. The predictions do not have to be exact or certain—we all know that there are mild winters, that harvests sometimes fail, buses break down and employers sometimes go bankrupt—but there has to be a degree of regularity and predictability or our social life would be impossible. A degree of predictability depends on a degree of determinism.

If both absolute determinism and absolute or strong indeterminism must be rejected this leaves relative determinism as the only practical option. If relative determinism is accepted as a general stance what we actually require from both natural and social science are theories which tell us what is determined and what is not and which establish for concrete situations the extent and limits of what is determined and the extent and limits of what can be altered by human decision and intervention. This is what is needed for everyday life, for farming the land, making goods and tools, planning a journey or driving a car. This is what is needed on a higher plane in a more systematic way for the project of consciously changing society.

Every course of political action, every strategic and tactical decision is dependent on judgements about what is and is not determined. For example: if the ideology of social groups is in no way determined by their economic position and class interest, then the utopian socialist project of persuading the ruling class of the virtues of a socialist society would be viable. If, on the other hand, the ideology of the individuals or social groups was mechanically and absolutely determined by their class interests there would be no point in trying to persuade anyone of anything, no point in any form of political argument or propaganda.

What Marxism provides better than any theory is precisely this: an account of what in human history and society is determined independent of our will and what it is possible to change through conscious intervention. It is this which makes Marxism 'not a dogma but a guide to action' in the struggle for workers' revolution and human liberation.

At this point it is necessary to note an apparent paradox. Provided one stops short of absolute determinism, which renders the concept of human freedom meaningless, determinism (in the theoretical sense) and freedom are not necessarily diversely related. On the contrary, the higher the level of human understanding of the natural and social forces that determine our lives, the more in practice is human choice and freedom expanded. For the uncomprehending, the laws of nature make it impossible to fly but a sophisticated understanding of those laws (along with the application of human labour) has made flight commonplace.

Another concept that needs signposting here is 'probabilistic determinism' (already mentioned in relation to quantum mechanics). Some things are very strongly determined and therefore virtually inevitable; some things are very probable but not certain; some things are likely; some things hang in the balance. Things which are only likely in individual cases become increasingly certain as the number of cases increases. It is certain that I will die. It is unlikely but not impossible that I will die tomorrow. It is probable but not certain that I will die before I reach 100. Given a million people it is virtually certain that the large majority die before the age of 100. If an individual middle class child is even marginally more likely to get to university than an individual working class child, it becomes virtually certain that a higher percentage of middle class children as a whole will go to university.

The concept of probabilistic determinism is politically important in at least three ways. First it plays a role in the current battle against ruling class ideology. The ruling class which is perfectly capable of grasping probabilistic determinism when it suits it (for instance when fixing insurance premiums) often denies it for propaganda purposes—as when rejecting a link between crime and unemployment. Secondly it is crucial in the understanding of history. Take the familiar question of the inevitability of the First World War. It makes no sense to argue that the outbreak of war was inevitable precisely at the beginning of August 1914. Princip might have missed his shot, the Austro-Hungarian government might have responded differently and so on. Nor should we be drawn into trying to prove the *absolute* inevitability of world war at some point. But it makes good sense to argue that given important rivalries the war was overwhelmingly likely (or virtually inevitable).

Thirdly it plays a central role in political tactics. The decision to call a strike or even a demonstration depends in considerable part on the assessment of the objective possibility of such an action taking place and being a success. Clearly there is no way in which such assessment can be rendered an exact science, but neither can it be dispensed with. Napoleon's oft quoted maxim, 'First engage, then we'll see', expresses an important truth, but only within definite limits. An army which engages in a pitched battle with an enemy that is better armed and many times its size will almost certainly be defeated, as will one which invades Russia without taking account of the highly deterministic effects of the Russian winter.

Finally it should be noted that, whereas absolute determinism renders conscious political action to change the world superfluous, and strong indeterminism renders it hopelessly ineffective, relative determinism puts a premium on such action. If in a given situation a particular desired outcome is either probable but not guaranteed or hangs in the balance, then every action taken towards that outcome (provided, of course, it is not counterproductive) increases the probability of it occurring and is therefore valuable. In the light of these theoretical considerations I shall now examine the extent and limits of determinism in the Marxist theory of history.

Forces and relations of production

Marx's theory of history begins with an assertion that is extremely simple and obvious:

> ...*that man must be in a position to live in order to be able to 'make history'. But life involves before everything else eating and drinking, a habitation, clothing and many other things.*[20]

Without food and water people die. This is so simple and obvious that one might wonder why Marx bothers with it (not once but repeatedly)[21] and why I bother to cite it. The answer is that it is a necessary first premise and that 'the writing of history must always set out from these natural bases',[22] but there are innumerable bourgeois theories and accounts of history and society which manage to lose sight of, conceal or evade this most fundamental point.

From the necessity for food, drink, clothing and so on, it follows, Marx argues, that the basis of every society and all human history is the production, through social labour, of these means of subsistence. This leads Marx to a further proposition:

In the social production of their life, men enter into definite relations that are indispensable and independent of their will, relations of production which correspond to a definite stage of development of their material productive forces.[23]

This is a proposition which can be summarised as the thesis that the level of development of the productive forces determines the social relations of production (provided we leave open for the moment the precise meaning of determine in this context).

There is no doubt that within the 'classical' interpretation of Marxism—the line that runs from Marx, through Engels, Lenin, Luxemburg and Trotsky—this thesis has been seen as a cornerstone of historical materialism. At the same time, however, every aspect of the proposition has been the subject of vigorous controversy, beginning with the meaning of the terms productive forces and relations of production.

Frequently the productive forces have been seen as simply the technology (tools/machinery) available to society—an interpretation which has served as the basis for viewing Marxism as essentially a theory of technological determinism. And certainly there is one passage in Marx which, taken in isolation, seems to support this interpretation, namely the famous statement in *The Poverty of Philosophy* that, 'The windmill gives you society with the feudal lord; the steam mill, society with the industrial capitalist'.[24] However, later in the same text Marx also writes that 'of all the instruments of production the greatest productive power is the revolutionary class itself'.[25] This suggests a broader interpretation of productive forces as not only machinery but also the labour of the producers. Quotations from Marx apart from this latter interpretation make far more sense for the simple reason that tools and machinery have first to be produced by human labour and, even then, do not produce anything themselves without further human labour to set them in motion. What is more, the labour involved is more than a matter of muscle power. The sophistication of technology clearly depends on the scientific knowledge of its makers, while in many areas of work skilled or educated labour is more productive than unskilled labour. The productive forces are therefore best defined as the general capacity to produce of a given society.

A similar choice exists between narrower and broader definitions of the relations of production. On this question, however, there have been three main positions. The first defines the relations of production as legal property relations. The second distinguishes between legal ownership and effective possession or control but still restricts the definition of relations of production to relations of effective possession or control of the means of production. The third sees relations of production as the totality of social relations into which individuals enter in the process of production.

The first position suffers from the serious defect of elevating form over content and appearance over reality and has proved a major obstacle to understanding the enormously important phenomenon of state capitalism either in its fully developed form in Russia or its partial form in Western nationalised industries. It should therefore be rejected.

The difference between the second and third positions is best brought into focus by looking at how each definition specifies the relations of production in capitalist society. According to the former the relations of production consist only of the relations between the capitalist class as owners or controllers of the means of production and employers of labour power and the working class as non-owners of the means of production and sellers of labour power. According to the latter they consist of these relations plus relations between workers and workers, between workers and supervisors, between supervisors and managers, between managers and owners, owners and owners and so on.

Here the narrower definition has the advantage of highlighting those social relations which are constitutive of capitalism as a system and of its fundamental classes—the bourgeoisie and proletariat, but it also has certain disadvantages. It can lead either to an oversimplified view of the class structure as consisting solely of capitalists and workers and no intermediate layers, or to a theorisation of those intermediate layers in terms of consumption and lifestyle rather than relations of production. It also leads to a remarkably static view of the relations of production in which these remain unchanged through centuries of economic development. Thus the enormous transformation from early industrial capitalism to contemporary multinational capitalism, from an economy dominated by relatively small individually owned and managed firms to one dominated by giant bureaucratically managed multinational corporations, would be held to involve no change in the relations of production. Such a conclusion stands in clear contradiction to Marx's famous statement in *The Communist Manifesto* that, 'The bourgeoisie cannot exist without constantly revolutionising the instruments of production, and thereby the relations of production, and with them the whole relations of society'.[26]

Finally there is the simple fact that relations between worker and worker, worker and supervisor and so on, clearly are social relations entered into in the process of production, ie relations of production.

For all these reasons it is preferable to adopt the wider and more flexible definition. In doing so, however, it is necessary to keep in mind the distinction between gradual quantitative shifts in the relations of production which do not change which class owns and controls the means of production and fundamental qualitative changes which do. The former changes affect the balance of power within a given mode of production. Only the latter mark the transition from one mode to another.

This brings us to the central question of the determination of the relations of production by the forces of production. As we have seen, Marx, in the 1859 *Preface*, writes of 'relations of production which correspond to a definite stage of development of these material productive forces.' He then argues that:

> At a certain stage in their development, the material productive forces of society come in conflict with the existing relations of production... From forms of development of the productive forces these relations turn into their fetters. Then begins an epoch of social revolution.[27]

However, this whole conception of the primacy of the forces of production has come under attack from various quarters. We have already mentioned what was historically the most significant of these attacks, that of Maoism. The Maoist claim to be constructing socialism, or even full communism, within the framework of the impoverished and predominantly rural country necessitated downplaying the significance of the productive forces. Thus the leading theoretician of Maoism in Europe, Charles Bettleheim, argued that, 'What is happening in China proves that a low level of development of the productive forces is no obstacle to a socialist transformation of social relations'.[28] In this case the denial of the primacy of the productive forces was associated with an extreme idealism and voluntarism which elevated the role of will power and political leadership in opposition to objective material conditions and social forces in a way that constituted a complete break with historical materialism in all but name. Moreover what happened in China proved that a low level of development of the productive forces was not only an obstacle to socialist transformation but even to the development of state capitalism in one country.

More surprising but also of more theoretical interest is the fact that Alex Callinicos in his *Marxism and Philosophy* has argued in favour of 'starting from the relations of production, and treating them, not the forces of production, as the independent variable'.[29] Alex appears to have come to this conclusion out of a desire to avoid the passive technological determinism of the Second International and the less passive but even more mechanical and dogmatic determinism of high Stalinism. In support of his position Callinicos cites Marx's account in *Capital* of how capitalist relations of production provided the impetus to the development of the productive forces which led to the industrial revolution. He also argues that the primacy of the productive forces derives from the early undeveloped formulation of historical materialism in *The German Ideology* rather than the mature version in the later works (with the 1859 *Preface* rejected as 'technological determinism' and 'to a large extent, a summary of *The German Ideology*').[30]

In fairness to Alex it should be said that he no longer holds this position. Nevertheless it is useful to consider these arguments and in considering them it is first of all necessary to recognise that the relations of production certainly do exert a powerful influence on the forces of production. This is both empirically verifiable and allowed for in Marx's classic formulation. The 1859 *Preface* indicates two possible kinds of influence of the relations on the forces of production: they can be 'forms of their development' (which I take to include positively encouraging their development) or they can become 'fetters' (ie they can restrict or hold back their development). Indeed Marx's analysis of the contradictions of capitalism—above all the tendency to overproduction and the tendency of the rate of profit to fall—shows that capitalist relations of production both drive the forces of production forwards and throw them backwards *simultaneously* with the development tendency predominating in times of booms and the 'fettering' tendency predominating in slumps, and the tendency towards slump increasing as the system ages.

Nevertheless there are strong reasons for continuing to assert the primacy of the productive forces and regarding the influence of the relations of productions as a secondary or derivative 'reaction back' upon the forces.[31] The most important reason is that if primacy is accorded to the relations of production then no explanation can be given for why the relations of production are what they are in any particular society or epoch. The concept of the relations of production is left, as it were, hanging in the air and the coherence of historical materialism as an overall theory of historical development is destroyed. In the process two other fundamental tenets of classical Marxism are undermined: the theory of revolution as rooted in the productive forces coming into conflict with the relations, and the theory that the fundamental economic prerequisite of socialism is the development of the productive forces to the point where it is possible to provide a decent life for all.[32] The same problem does not arise, however, if the forces of production are seen as primary since both the existence and growth of the productive forces are explained, in the final analysis, by the struggle to meet biologically given human needs, which are themselves the product of natural evolution.

An additional argument in favour of this position is that it conforms to the large majority of the classic accounts of historical materialism by Marx and Engels, not only in the 1859 *Preface* and *The German Ideology* but also in *The Poverty of Philosophy*, *The Communist Manifesto*, *Anti-Dühring*, *The Origin of the Family, Private Property and the State* and elsewhere. Even the quotation from *Capital* chosen by Alex as favourable to his position contains a reference to the ultimate priority of the productive forces which is very similar to the formulation in the 1859 *Preface*:

> *It is always the direct relationship of the owners of the conditions of production to the direct producers—**a relation always naturally corresponding to a definite stage in the methods of labour and thereby its social productivity**—which reveals the innermost secret, the hidden basis of the entire social structure.*[33] [my emphasis]

Finally Chris Harman has provided persuasive theoretical and empirical backing for the primacy of the productive forces in relation to the important test case of the transition from feudalism to capitalism. The influential American Marxist Robert Brenner has argued that this transition is to be explained primarily in terms of the class struggle in the countryside between lords and peasants (ie relations of production) rather than the development of trade, industry and the bourgeoisie in the towns (forces of production). In opposition both to Brenner and the earlier theories of Pirenne, Sweezy and Wallerstein, Harman draws on the work of Le Geff, Kriedle and other historians to vindicate—in more developed form—Marx's account of 'the way in which the growth of the forces of production within feudalism threw up new relations of production, relations which came into collision with the old society and led to bourgeois revolution...centred in the towns...reinforced by the revolt of the rural classes'.[34]

But if the productive forces are primary and their state of development must be the point of departure for all Marxist historical analysis, their relationship to the relations of production cannot be one of mechanical or automatic determination. Any notion of automatic determination here is refuted by the historical fact of social revolution since social revolution involves precisely a radical transformation of the relations of production on the basis of a given level of development of the productive forces. In Russia the relations of production in 1918 were substantially different from those which had existed in 1916 while the productive forces had, if anything, declined. Moreover Marx's concept of the forces of production coming into conflict with the existing relations of production would be impossible if there were absolute or mechanical determination of relations of forces. Clearly, therefore, we are again in the realm of relative determinism. The nature of this relative determinism is, I believe, best understood as a combination of constraint and impulse.

On the one hand the level of development of the productive forces sets definite limits to the relations of production possible at a given point of time. Thus in the earliest stages of human history, when the forces of production restricted human beings to nomadic hunting and gathering, exploitative relations of production (ie the division of society into classes) were excluded. The productive forces in Europe in the 11th century, however, excluded the possibility of either primitive communist or modern socialist relations of production. The population (itself a force of production) had long since far exceeded the number that could be supported by hunting and gathering, and surplus was being generated which permitted the ruling class to maintain armed forces easily able to crush any experiment in primitive egalitarianism. At the same time the productive forces were sufficient to support a decent life only for a tiny minority: no matter how production was organised or goods distributed it was not possible to liberate the population as a whole from poverty, hunger and a life of endless toil. In contrast the productive forces in contemporary society exclude either primitive communist or feudal relations of production: they permit only capitalist or socialist relations or, to be exact, relations transitional to socialism.

On the other hand the development of the productive forces in Europe from, at least, the 15th century onwards generated a powerful impulse to the rise of capitalist relations of production developing, as Marx put it, 'in the interstices of feudal society'. From the early 19th century onwards the development of the productive forces has created an increasingly powerful impulse towards socialism. The increasing socialisation of production, the growth of the world working class, the rise of the world economy, the advances of science and technology (with their immense potential for destruction as well as construction) all press humanity in the direction of social ownership and democratic planning.

However, historical experience has demonstrated conclusively that the development of the productive forces is not in itself enough to determine the transition from one mode of production to another, either from feudalism to capitalism or from capitalism to socialism. It is a necessary but not sufficient condition. For such a transition to occur it is also necessary that a new social class (the rise of which is both determined by, and part of, the growth of the productive forces) should actually overthrow the old ruling class (which owes its position to the old mode of production and has a vested interest in its preservation) and wrest state power from its hands. It is in this sense that the class struggle is the loco-motive of history.

Base and superstructure

At this point it is possible to make some general comments on the much debated question of the determination of the superstructure of society by the economic base. Speaking at Marx's graveside Engels stated:

> *Just as Darwin discovered the law of development of organic nature so Marx discovered the law of the development of human history: the simple fact, hith-erto concealed by an overgrowth of ideology, that mankind must first of all eat, drink, have shelter and clothing before it can pursue politics, science, art, religion etc, and therefore the production of the immediate material means of subsistence and consequently the degree of economic development attained by a given people or during a given epoch from the foundation upon which the state institutions, the legal conceptions, art, and even the ideas on religion of the people concerned, have been evolved, and in the light of which they must, therefore, be explained, instead of vice versa, as had hitherto been the case.*[35]

The insistence on the primacy of the economic base in relation to the superstructure, on the explanation of the latter by the former 'instead of vice versa', on the determination of consciousness by social being, not being by consciousness, is common to all the classic accounts of histor-ical materialism by its founders and is clearly fundamental to Marxism as a whole.

Yet in noting this we should also observe that in the large majority of these statements Marx and Engels formulate the relationship between superstructure and base in terms of 'correspondence', 'conditioning', or 'arising from' rather than strict determination. Thus in the 1859 *Preface* we find:

> *...the economic structure of society, the real basis on which **rises** a legal and political superstructure and to which **correspond** definite forms of social con-sciousness. The mode of production of material life **conditions** the social, political and intellectual life process in general...*
>
> *With the change of the economic foundation the entire immense super-structure is **more or less** rapidly transformed.* [my emphasis—JM][36]

Moreover Engels, in his late letters, repeatedly stresses that neither he nor Marx intended to suggest a mechanical or absolute determination of the superstructure by the base:

*According to the materialist conception of history the **ultimately** determining element in history is the production and reproduction of real life. More than this neither Marx nor I have ever asserted. Hence if somebody twists this into saying that the economic element is the **only** determining one, he transforms that proposition into a meaningless, abstract, senseless phrase. The economic situation is the basis, but the various elements of the superstructure—political forms of the class struggle and its results, to wit: constitutions established by the victorious class after successful battle, etc, judicial forms and then even the reflexes of all these actual struggles in the brains of the participants, political, juristic, philosophical theories, religious views and their further development into systems of dogmas—also exercise their influence upon the course of the historical struggles and in many cases preponderate in determining their form.[37]*

In *The Eighteenth Brumaire of Louis Bonaparte* Marx himself gives vivid expression to the way in which ideas can outlive the economic and social conditions from which they arose:

The tradition of all the dead generations weighs like a nightmare on the brain of the living. And just when they seem engaged in revolutionising themselves and things, in creating something that has never yet existed, precisely in such periods of revolutionary crisis they anxiously conjure up the spirits of the past to their service and borrow from them names, battle cries and costumes in order to present the new scene of world history in this time honoured disguise and this borrowed language.[38]

And in his Preface to *The History of the Russian Revolution* Trotsky draws the connection between this absence of mechanical determinism and the fact of revolution:

The point is that society does not change its institutions as need arises, the way a mechanic changes his instruments. On the contrary, society actually takes the institutions which hung upon it as given for once for all.

The swift changes of mass views and moods in an epoch of revolution thus derive not from the flexibility and mobility of man's mind, but just the opposite, from its deep conservativism. The chronic lag of ideas and relations behind new objective conditions, right up to the moment when the latter crash over people in the form of a catastrophe, is what creates in a period of revolution that leaping movement of ideas and passions which seems to the police mind a mere result of the activities of 'demagogues'.[39]

It is therefore clear that any charge against Marxism of mechanical or crude economic determinism completely misses the mark. On the question of base and superstructure, as on the question of forces and relations of production, what historical materialism stands for is relative determinism and the concepts of constraint and impulse are again applicable.

On the one hand the nature of the economic base sets definite limits to the nature of the superstructure so that, for example, a feudal base is incompatible with universal suffrage and parliamentary democracy and obviously could not give rise to the philosophy of John Stuart Mill, the economics of Adam Smith, the novel as the dominant literary form or the paintings of either Rembrandt or Jackson Pollock. On the other hand developments in the base, both in the forces and the relations of production, continually generate pressures for change in the superstructure. Thus the first stirrings of capitalism in Europe generated pressures for a challenge to the Catholic Church which was both a major feudal landowner in its own right and provided ideological legitimation for the feudal order as a whole. The eventual outcome of these pressures was the Reformation in the 16th century and the emergence with Calvinism of a new form of Christianity favourable to the needs of early capitalist accumulation. While the Industrial Revolution in Britain provided an impulse for the enfranchisement, first, of the industrial bourgeoisie and middle class, and then, of the industrial working class (resulting in the Reform Acts of 1832, 1867 and 1884). Similarly a change in the base—the massive rise in paid employment of women during the post-war economic boom—provided the impulse for a significant, though partial, change in the dominant social attitude towards women. Though, it must immediately be added, none of these impulses were realised automatically or without bitter conflict, the outcome of which might have been different.

At this point we can consider the difficult and complex question of the extent to which different elements of the superstructure are more or less strictly determined by the base. In general it can be said that those elements of the superstructure which have immediate practical implications such as the law, the judiciary, the police, the military, the education system and so on are more closely tied to the base and in particular to the economic interests of the ruling class than are the more ideological elements such as religious doctrines, philosophy and art. Thus a modern capitalist economy could not coexist with laws which were anti-capitalist in that they either looked back to feudalism by, for example, prohibiting usury (lending money and charging interest) or anticipated socialism by banning the employment of wage labour or legalising the expropriation of the rich by the poor. A capitalist economy can, however, coexist with art that yearns for the feudal past (the Pre-Raphaelites in Victorian England, the poetry of Ezra Pound, the fantasy novels of J R R Tolkien) or makes propaganda for the socialist future (the plays of Brecht, the paintings of Leger and so on). It is also possible to differentiate between art forms with architecture, for example, more directly influenced and more strictly limited by economics than poetry. Certainly capitalism can and does coexist with a wide variety of religions that long predate capitalism in their origins (though of course to survive the religions have to adapt themselves to capitalism).

However, all such generalisations require substantial qualification. Engels takes great care to explain the relative autonomy of the legal sphere:

> *As soon as the new division which creates lawyers becomes necessary another new and independent sphere is opened up which, for all its general dependence on production and trade, still has a special capacity for reacting upon these spheres. In a modern state, law must not only correspond to the general economic condition and be its expression but also must be an **internally coherent** expression which does not, owing to inner contradictions, reduce itself to nought. And in order to achieve this the faithful reflection of economic conditions suffers increasingly.*[40]

Similarly Marx's analysis of Bonapartism and Trotsky's of fascism deal with situations in which the capitalist state machine passes out of the direct control of the capitalist class and can therefore impose certain policies which are not in the interests of that class: for example, the Nazi Holocaust which cannot be accounted for by either the economic or political needs of the German bourgeoisie.[41]

Whereas in philosophy and art many of the finest achievements derive their greatness precisely from their close relationship to the economic base. Marxism itself is an example of this in that its power consists not in its autonomy or detachment but in its accurate reflection of the fundamental contradictions in the economic basis of society and its exact expression of the interests of the main productive force in society, namely the proletariat.[42] In art one can cite such paintings as Rembrandt's numerous portraits of the newly ascendant Dutch bourgeoisie (for example *The Anatomy Lesson of Dr Tulp*, *The Night Watch*, and *The Syndics*) or Turner's *Rain, Steam and Speed* which dramatically evokes that great driving force of 19th century capitalism, the locomotive, or the manifestos, poems and paintings of the Futurists which self consciously celebrate the arrival of the automobile, electricity and the 20th century metropolis, while in literature the novels of Defoe, Austen, Balzac and Dickens (to name but a few) all show a direct relationship to economic and social developments.

Clearly, however, it is a consequence of the relative determinist position that in the whole area of base and superstructure and particularly in the ideological sphere all generalisations, all schema—though necessary—are of only limited value and must rapidly make way for concrete analysis.

Laws of motion of capitalism

One significant aspect of the overall problem of determinism and of base and superstructure is the extent of the determination of human behaviour by the economic laws of motion of capitalism. The fact that Marx devoted the major part of his life to laying bare these laws in his master work, *Capital*, shows that he considered them to be of the highest importance in shaping contemporary and future human actions. Moreover the very notion of an economic law of motion implies a high level of determinism.

In fact when it comes to the *economic* behaviour of individuals and even more so of classes, Marxism is at its *most* deterministic. Marxism insists that the working class as a whole has no choice but to sell its labour power to the employers[43] and little choice about which employer it sells it to. Equally it insists that capitalists, and capitalist managers, have, because of competition, no choice but to strive to maximise their accumulation of capital and therefore to maximise their rate of exploitation. It argues that the values of commodities, including the value of labour power, and therefore, in the long run, their prices, are objectively rather than subjectively determined and are certainly not arbitrary.[44]

It argues further that competitive capital accumulation on the basis of the laws of value leads inevitably to a tendency for the rate of profit to decline,[45] which in turn leads to economic crisis in the form of recessions of increasing frequency and severity.

The validity or otherwise of Marxist economic analysis and its theory of crisis cannot be debated here.[46] I merely wish to stress its highly deterministic character.

Even here we are not talking of absolute or mechanical determinism. Individual workers may become new age travellers or full time revolutionaries. Individual capitalists may become philanthropists and certainly make serious errors in their pursuit of profit. Various factors, foreseen and unforeseen, can counteract the falling rate of profit and thus defer the crisis.[47] There is nothing in Marxist theory which can totally exclude the possibility of a cosmic accident upsetting the whole process. Nevertheless the element of determinism in this area is clearly very strong.

This strong determinism with regard to the laws of motion of capitalism leads to a point of sharp political conflict between Marxism and all varieties of reformism. Reformists of all stripes believe, or at least say they believe, that governments staffed by people of goodwill and sagacity (namely themselves) will be able, without first overthrowing capitalist relations of production, to manipulate the working of the capitalist economy so as to cure its crisis, moderate its exploitation and generally make it work in the interests of working people. Marxists argue that this is a disastrous illusion and that the economic laws of capitalism are far stronger than the good intentions of reformist politicians.

Confronted with the realities of the capitalist economy reformist governments either (and this is the most common scenario) surrender their programmes for reform and meekly adapt themselves to capitalist priorities or if, under mass pressure from below, they are more stubborn, are rapidly thrown into chaos and disarray. The one thing they are not able to do is substantially modify either the logic of the system or its tendency to crisis. Once again this is not the place to argue in any detail the Marxist case on the question of social democratic governments. Suffice to say that the historical record—including the record of seven Labour governments in Britain since 1924, of the Weimar Republic, of Popular Unity in Chile, of Mitterrand in France and Gonzalez in Spain—testifies strongly in favour of Marxist determinism.

Yet at the same time as emphasising this determining power of the laws of motion of capitalism Marxism also takes, at a different level of the argument, an anti-deterministic position with regard to those laws. The general tendency among outright supporters and ideologists of capitalism—its professional economists, politicians and so on, and among capitalists themselves, is to treat these laws, laws of the market as they call them, as eternal and unchanging. Sometimes they are seen directly as laws of nature—it was Margaret Thatcher who said, 'You can no more defy the laws of the market than you can defy the laws of gravity.' Alternatively they are seen as emanating from a timeless and fixed human nature—the selfish, atomised, benefit maximising *homo economicus* of the classical economists. Either way they are presented as outside, and beyond, any possibility of human control and any attempt to resist or challenge them is depicted as simultaneously utopian, harmful and wicked.

Marxism rejects this. It maintains that contemporary economic laws derive neither from nature nor human nature but exclusively from capitalist relations of production which are a product of history, ie of past human actions, and which can be changed by human action. As long as capitalist relations of production remain in place, however, the laws of motion of capitalism will remain in operation and will, in the long run, prevail over all opposition and resistance.[48]

Before leaving the question of the determining role of the laws of capitalism it is necessary to consider the relative freedom of action of the different social classes. Here we confront an apparent paradox. When it is a matter of personal or individual behaviour it is obvious that members of the capitalist class have vastly more freedom than members of the working class. They can dwell, holiday, eat, drink and play where they want. By contrast workers have little or no choice in these areas. But when it comes to social and political action, to action as a class, there is a vital sense in which the working class is freer, less determined, than the bourgeoisie. Historically the bourgeoisie are locked into the system they preside over, prisoners of both its drive to accumulate and its contradictions. They are at home in their alienation, and, as Marx puts it, 'the capitalist is merely capital personified and functions in the process of production solely as the agent of capital'.[49] The working class, however, can and does resist the imperatives of capital. And, from the moment they resist, workers become more than mere personifications of labour power. They make a start on the road to the transcendence of their alienation and to becoming conscious directors of production, society and history.

The contrast between the captivity of the bourgeoisie and the (relative) freedom of the proletariat also has implications for the intermediate strata commonly referred to as the middle class. Within the left wing of this layer the political strategy of reformism is intimately connected with the personal strategy of advancement up the hierarchy of the professions and institutions. The social worker, the local government officer, the teacher and the journalist tell themselves and others that they have to rise through the management structure to run their department, school, paper or whatever so as to put their ideas into practice and have the power to change things. In reality the higher the individual rises the more they become circumscribed by the logic of capital, the more they lose their freedom to oppose that logic, and in that sense the more determined their behaviour becomes.

Determinism and the class struggle

The greater relative freedom of the proletariat, its ability to choose to resist the imperatives of capital, leads directly to the question of determinism and the class struggle. To what extent is the existence, course and outcome of the class struggle objectively determined independently of the will, consciousness and deliberate intervention of workers and revolutionary socialists? This question or series of questions is politically the most important aspect of the whole question of determinism. It is the point at which the philosophical debate bears most directly on socialist practice.

It is, of course, one of the central pillars of historical materialism that the class struggle throughout history derives from exploitative relations of production. Indeed it is exploitation, the appropriation of surplus labour extorted from the immediate producers, which generates the conflict in which class struggle takes shape. As G E M de Ste Croix has put it, 'Class (essentially a relationship) is the collective social expression of the fact of exploitation, the way in which exploitation is embodied in a social structure.'[50] In capitalist society it is the extraction of surplus value hidden within the relationship of wage labour which gives rise to the antagonism and struggle between the bourgeoisie and proletariat. There is an objective conflict of interests between the classes in which the capitalists, driven by competition, strive continually to increase the rate of exploitation (by lowering wages, extending the working day and increasing productivity) and the workers, driven by naturally given and socially developed needs, strive to restrict it. This is a battle which goes on every working day of every working week in every workplace throughout the capitalist world and throughout the capitalist epoch and which, in more or less mediated form, permeates every other aspect and level of society. The existence of class struggle is therefore not something invented, created, stirred up or otherwise brought into being by Marx or Marxists, or agitators or troublemakers. It is an economically determined and inevitable feature of capitalist society.

The level of intensity of the class struggle, however, varies enormously. Bourgeois society passes through periods of apparent class peace when class conflict, though continuing, is buried beneath the surface and through periods of open class warfare in the literal sense of revolution and civil war, and through every intermediate level between these extremes.

In analysing the extent to which the level of the class struggle is economically or otherwise determined it is necessary briefly to return to the distinction made earlier between the relative freedom of action of the bourgeoisie and proletariat. The bourgeois and proletarian sides of the class struggle are obviously interrelated but they are not identical or exactly symmetrical. The bourgeois side is strongly economically determined. Clearly political, historical and even individual psychological factors do play a part in influencing both the tactics and ferocity with which it pursues its interests. Nevertheless the compulsion of economics is very powerful and the bourgeoisie has developed a very strong 'class instinct', ie a very clear practical awareness of where its interests lie. It is therefore possible to formulate the general rule or 'law' that in times of economic crisis when profit rates fall and competition between capitals intensifies the bourgeoisie will step up its assault on working class living standards.

However, when it comes to the proletarian side we cannot say, à la Newton, that every (bourgeois) action meets with an equal and opposite reaction. It is an empirical fact that there has always been resistance to exploitation and oppression even in the most difficult circumstances (even in Nazi Germany and Stalinist Russia, even in the death camps and the gulag). But it is no less a fact that there is always also acquiescence and even collaboration. The relative proportions of these different responses vary enormously and not in any fixed or mechanical relationship to economic conditions.

Clearly the level of development of the productive forces, and their accompanying relations of production, together with the immediate economic conjuncture constitute the point of departure for the level of working class struggle. The degree and nature of industrialisation in a society determines the size of the working class and its objective weight within the economy. It thus also determines the *potential* strength of the working class in struggle but what it does not, in itself, determine is the extent to which this potential will actually be realised. In the early years of this century the working class in economically advanced Germany and Britain were larger and potentially more powerful than the working class in backward Russia but the level of struggle in Russia was much higher. The immediate economic situation can provide powerful impulses to struggle—inflation, for example, is a strong impetus to the fight for higher wages—but again the response is not automatic.

Trotsky discussed this question on a number of occasions.[51] He argued that the rise of a mass revolutionary workers' movement and a successful struggle for state power were undoubtedly premised on a generalised crisis of the capitalist order, ie an exacerbation of the fundamental contradiction between the forces and relations of production which produces a prolonged period of instability and rapid alteration of booms and slumps. But he rejects the idea of any 'automatic dependence of the proletarian revolutionary movement upon a crisis. There is only dialectical interaction'.[52] In particular Trotsky stresses how in certain circumstances, especially where the working class is exhausted after major battles, prolonged unemployment can demoralise and weaken its struggles, whereas a temporary economic revival can raise the level of struggle.

> *In contrast, the industrial revival is bound, first of all, to raise the self-confidence of the working class, undermined by failures and by disunity in its own ranks: it is bound to fuse the working class together in the factories and plants and heighten desire for unanimity in militant actions.[53]*
>
> *...At the moment when the factory stops discharging old workers and takes on new ones, the self-confidence of the workers is strengthened: they are once again necessary.[54]*

These observations are extremely useful pointers or guidelines but can no more be treated as universally valid generalisations than the mechanical notion that slump equals revolt. Firstly because even in purely economic terms no two booms and no two slumps are the same. Secondly because the relationship between economic conditions and workers' struggle is mediated by numerous factors—the level and quality of trade union organisation, the level and quality of political organisation, the level of general political consciousness, the level of anger, the behaviour of trade union and political leadership, and the strength, confidence, cleverness and so on, of the capitalist class—all of which are conditioned not only by the current situation but also by the immediate and even by the more distant past, and all of which are involved in a complex interaction.

Thus any satisfactory account of the level and course of the class struggle either in the past or the present must be a concrete analysis which takes economic conditions as its starting point but includes all these elements. The complexity of this means that any attempt to predict the shape of working class struggle even in the immediate future, and certainly beyond, must be undertaken with great caution. Gramsci's warning is salutary:

> In reality one can 'scientifically' foresee only the struggle, but not the concrete moments of the struggle which cannot but be the result of opposing forces in continuous movements which are never reducible to fixed quantities since within them quantity is continuously becoming quality.[55]

However, the ultimate purpose of all Marxist analysis of the class struggle is neither to predict its future nor to provide an adequate explanation of its history, but to intervene in it so as to help shape its direction. And it is precisely from the standpoint of intervention that the level of the class struggle must within certain limits be regarded, by either the individual socialist militant or the revolutionary party, as given, ie as objectively determined independently of the will of the individual or the party. As every shop steward or union rep knows (or soon learns) strikes cannot be called at will in the absence of a genuine wish to fight on the part of the workers concerned. This applies even more strongly to general strikes or insurrections and any violation of this law of revolutionary strategy invariably has disastrous consequences. (The classic negative example of this rule is the March Action of 1921 in which the German Communist Party artificially attempted to goad the German working class into revolution and succeeded only in shattering its own membership and authority).[56] By the same token there are times when sections of the working class or even the majority of the class move into struggle regardless of the objections or reservations of even its most advanced leaders. Such a movement was the February Revolution of 1917 when the mass revolt that overthrew Tsarism began, despite an initially reluctant Bolshevik Party. As Trotsky records:

> The 23rd of February was International Women's Day. The social-democratic circles had intended to mark this day in a general manner: by meetings,

speeches, leaflets. It had not occurred to anyone that it might become the first day of the revolution. Not a single organisation called for strikes on this day. What is more, even a Bolshevik organisation, and a most militant one—the Vyborg borough-committee, all workers—was opposing strikes.

...On the following morning, however, in spite of all directives, the women textile workers in several factories went on strike and sent delegates to the metal workers with an appeal for support...

Thus the fact is that the February Revolution was begun from below, over-coming the resistance of its own revolutionary organisations...[57]

In both these sets of circumstances would-be revolutionary leaders of local or national level have first to adjust themselves to objectively determined reality.

This recognition of necessity is, however, only the starting point of action. Leadership designed to focus the struggle, and raise its level further, is necessary to ensure its success. It is equally part of the experience of every rank and file militant and every political leadership that there are moments when a single speech at a mass meeting, a bold lead by a shop stewards committee or a concerted intervention by a political party can make a significant or even decisive difference to the course of the struggle, either positively or negatively. Thus the decision of the NUM and TUC leadership in October 1992 to march the first great demonstration against pit closures around Hyde Park rather than leading it directly to parliament made an immense difference to the ability of the Tory government to ride out that crisis. Conversely the decision, or rather series of decisions, by the Socialist Workers Party in 1977 to confront the National Front at Lewisham, and to launch the Anti Nazi League, made an enormous difference to the struggle against fascism in Britain.

This brings us to the question of whether the final outcome of the class struggle can be regarded as determined, that is to the old question of the 'inevitability of socialism'. It has to be admitted that there has been a certain ambiguity in this question within the classical Marxist tradition. Even in *The Communist Manifesto* itself we find conflicting formulations. On the one hand:

What the bourgeoisie therefore produces, above all, are its own gravediggers. Its fall and the victory of the proletariat are equally inevitable.[58]

On the other:

The history of all hitherto existing society is the history of class struggle...a fight that each time ended, either in a revolutionary reconstitution of society at large or in the common ruin of the contending classes.[59]

Of course there is an element of rhetorical flourish in that 'equally inevitable' just as there is a lack of specificity in 'the common ruin of the contending classes'. But nearly 150 years on from the *Manifesto* the rhetoric of inevitability has a hollow ring whereas the concrete form of 'common ruin' has become all too clear. From the moment capitalism armed itself with nuclear weapons and thus demonstrated its capacity to destroy itself and humanity with it, talk of the inevitability of socialism became absurd.[60]

However, it is not just a question of the possibility of nuclear holocaust, the experience of 20th century workers' revolutions has demonstrated the same point. After the Russian Revolution, the German Revolution, the Spanish Revolution and others it is palpably false to see socialist revolution as a wholly determined or guaranteed process. To acknowledge this is not to reduce socialism to a utopia or to regard the victory of the working class as a matter of chance. On the contrary, as Marxism has always argued, there are powerful and objectively determined historical forces working in favour of proletarian victory. These include: its immense numerical superiority over the bourgeoisie; its concentration in workplaces and in cities; the dependence of the bourgeoisie on the working class for all its operations including the operation of its state; and the fact that the working class can rule society without the bourgeoisie but the bourgeoisie cannot exist without the working class, which means that the bourgeoisie has to go on defeating the working class indefinitely but the proletariat has only to defeat the bourgeoisie once (in the world historical sense). These factors make the eventual victory of the the proletariat a realistic possibility. They may even make it probable. However they do not guarantee it.

They do not guarantee it because in order to make the transition from subordinate to ruling class the proletariat has to pass through an acute confrontation with the bourgeoisie, in which, for a period, the power of the two classes is almost equal and at which point the bourgeoisie, if given the chance, will strike back at the working class with tremendous force. At this point, therefore, history can go either way. Trotsky, writing on the eve of Hitler's triumph in Germany, used a striking metaphor to describe such a situation.

Germany is now passing through one of those great historic hours upon which the fate of the German people, the fate of Europe, and in significant measure the fate of all humanity, will depend for decades. If you place a ball on top of a pyramid, the slightest impact can cause it to roll down either to the left or to the right. That is the situation approaching with every hour in Germany today. There are forces which would like the ball to roll down towards the right and break the back of the working class. There are forces which would like the ball to remain at the top. That is utopia. The ball cannot remain at the top of the pyramid. The Communists want the ball to roll down toward the left and break the back of capitalism.[61]

The Russian Revolution passed through just such a moment in September and October of 1917. The counter-revolution in the shape of General Kornilov had attempted to drown the revolution in blood and had been repulsed. It was preparing to strike again. The Bolsheviks had won a majority in the Soviets and the working class was looking to them to turn their words into deeds. The Provisional Government under Kerensky was paralysed and crumbling. The fate of the revolution was poised on a knife edge between the dictatorship of the proletariat and the dictatorship of the counter-revolution.

No one understood this better than Lenin. In a remarkable series of speeches, articles and letters Lenin bombarded the Central Committee of the Bolshevik Party with ever more urgent demands that they 'seize the time' and organise the insurrection. The theme of these texts, repeated again and again, is that the revolution has reached a decisive turning point and that 'procrastination is like unto death'.[62] On 29 September, 1917 Lenin writes:

> *The crisis has matured. The whole future of the Russian Revolution is at stake. The honour of the Bolshevik Party is in question. The future of the international workers' revolution for socialism is at stake...*
>
> *To refrain from seizing power now, to 'wait'...is to **doom the revolution to failure**.*[63] [emphasis in original].

On 24 October he writes:

> *The situation is critical in the extreme...*
>
> *I exhort my comrades with all my heart and strength to realise that everything now hinges on a thread... The government is wavering. It must be destroyed at all costs!*
>
> *To delay will be fatal.*[64]

Reflecting on this episode, and also on the equally crucial 'April Days' when Lenin reoriented the Bolshevik Party away from the idea of completing the bourgeois revolution and in favour of soviet power, Trotsky concluded that Lenin's role in the victory of the revolution had been indispensable. Without Lenin, he wrote, 'there would have been no October Revolution; the leadership of the Bolshevik Party would have prevented it from occurring'.[65]

The significance of this conclusion for the question of determinism as a whole is brought out by Isaac Deutscher who criticises Trotsky on pre-

cisely this point. In *The Prophet Outcast* Deutscher charges Trotsky with
exaggerating the role of Lenin, with succumbing, in this instance, to the
Lenin 'cult' and with presenting an argument, 'which goes strongly
against the grain of the Marxist intellectual tradition'.[66] He cites as his
authority, and as 'highly representative of that tradition', Plekhanov's
The Role of the Individual in History which argues that 'influential individuals can change *the individual features of events and some of their
particular consequence* but they cannot change their general *trend* which
is determined by other forces'[67] [emphasis in original].

On the specifics of the issue the evidence strongly favours Trotsky in
that it is extremely unlikely that any other revolutionary leader in Russia
in 1917 could have done what Lenin did, ie win the Bolshevik leadership
to an insurrectionary perspective.[68] But what is important is that the logic
of the Plekhanov/Deutscher argument extends beyond the particular case
of Lenin to the whole historical role of party leadership, for it was not as
an individual inspirer of the masses that Lenin made his decisive contribution but in and through the Bolshevik Party. As I have written
elsewhere:

> *If the decisions or influence of individuals cannot be decisive then what of the
> decisions of party leaderships, which are made up of individuals or indeed
> parties as a whole, which compared to the basic forces of revolution, ie
> classes, are still relatively small groups? Deutscher believes that such a view
> contradicts the fundamental Marxist view that major historical changes are
> effected by mass social forces. What he misses is the dialectical point that his-
> torical development is the product of contradiction, of great social forces
> moving in **opposite** directions and that at key historical turning points these
> social forces may balance each other almost exactly.*
>
> *It is precisely in such situations that apparently small factors such as the
> quality of leadership or the decisions of a central committee can decisively
> shift the balance and therefore the course of history one way or the other.
> What is dangerous about the deterministic view is that it is only in such situ-
> ations of balance that the proletarian revolution can occur. Unlike the
> bourgeoisie, the proletariat cannot steadily accumulate strength until it is
> economically, politically and culturally more powerful than its adversary. Its
> situation as a toiling, exploited and propertyless class means that a situation
> of 'balance' is the best and the highest position that the proletariat can
> achieve under capitalism. If that 'moment' is lost the power of the bour-
> geoisie and capital will inevitably reassert itself.[69]*

Plekhanov and Deutscher stand here, as elsewhere, as representatives
of a strongly determinist interpretation of Marxism which slides all too

easily into passive fatalism and which it is one of the main purposes of this article to reject.[70]

Further confirmation of the anti-determinist position is provided by the fate of the German Revolution. The German Revolution, viewed as an overall process, lasted five years from the end of 1918 to the end of 1923, but it was in 1923 that it came to a head. In the summer and autumn of that year all the objective forces making for an acute revolutionary situation came together: a generalised economic, social and political crisis greatly sharpened by the French occupation of the Ruhr, leading to catastrophic inflation; sudden and massive pauperisation of the majority of the population; a large and powerful working class movement; a rapid disillusionment with the reformist leaders and organisations; a massive spontaneous strike wave; a mass revolutionary party (the KPD) rapidly gaining the support of the majority of the working class. And yet this outstanding revolutionary opportunity was allowed to go begging. The KPD failed throughout the summer of 1923 to draw up any coherent plan of action for the struggle for power or to give a strong revolutionary lead. Continuously looking to Moscow for advice, it continued its vacillation between forming local coalition governments with social democrats and playing with insurrection right through to the fiasco of an isolated uprising of a few hundred Communists in Hamburg in October which was crushed in 48 hours. As Trotsky observed, 'We witnessed in Germany a classic demonstration of how it is possible to miss a perfectly exceptional revolutionary situation of world-historic importance'.[71]

It is impossible to explain the victory in Russia and the defeat in Germany by means of a theory of absolute economic or social determinism. The difference lay in the subjective factor, the quality of revolutionary leadership, in that Heinrick Brandler and the other leaders of the KPD failed to take the initiative at the crucial moment. Of course, with hindsight, it is possible to offer reasons why the German leadership failed—they were being restrained and misadvised by Zinoviev (and Stalin) in Moscow; they were demoralised and conservative as a result of their mistakes in the March action. However, the interrogation of each of these reasons leads back to events and circumstances that could easily have been different: if Lenin had not suffered a stroke and had been in command in Moscow; if the Russian leadership had acceded to Brandler's request that Trotsky should go to Germany; if Luxemburg, by far the greatest of the KPD leaders, had not been murdered in 1919. But to accept the possibility of revolutionary victory in Germany in 1923 is to accept the possibility that subsequent world history would have been completely different—no fascism in Germany, no Stalinism in Russia and the real possibility of world revolution.[72]

To summarise, we can say that on the question of class struggle
Marxism takes the same relative determinist position that was argued for
on abstract grounds earlier in this article. It treats the existence of the
class struggle as extremely strongly determined, its general level as
strongly but by no means completely determined and its final outcome as
hanging in the balance.

However, it hangs in the balance between strongly determined alternatives, ultimately between socialism and barbarism. Capitalism is of
course continuously barbaric—think of the Somme, Auschwitz,
Hiroshima, the Gulf War, Rwanda and many other examples—but in the
socialist tradition the term barbarism has another, related but distinct,
meaning. 'It may denote the total destruction of civilisation by the
decline of society into an ahistorical era'[73] or Marx's 'common ruin of
the contending classes'. It is in the latter sense that I use it here, for the
highly determined dynamic and contradictions of capitalism are such
that if capitalism is allowed to survive indefinitely it will destroy us all.

This analysis has very clear implications for socialist practice. It
means that in every concrete situation there is a definite limit on what we
by our conscious action can achieve. At the same time every action, no
matter how small, which assists the working class struggle also con-
tributes, albeit only in small measure, to making its eventual victory
more likely. By far the most effective action that socialists can take is to
combine and co-ordinate their efforts in a political party which both
works to advance the class struggle to the maximum in the here and now
and prepares for the moment or moments of decisive confrontation in the
future.

Clearly it is not possible to 'arrange' in advance to have a Lenin, or a
Trotsky or a Luxemburg present at the appropriate time, but building a
strong revolutionary party is still the most, or rather the only, effective
way of achieving an effective leadership. For as Lenin writes:

> It is, in fact, one of the functions of a party organisation and of party leaders
> worthy of the name, to acquire, through the prolonged, persistent, variegated
> and comprehensive efforts of all thinking representatives of a given class, the
> knowledge, experience and—in addition to knowledge and experience—the
> political flair necessary for the speedy and correct solution of complex polit-
> ical problems.[74]

And as Trotsky put it:

> Bolshevism is not a doctrine (ie not merely a doctrine) but a system of revolu-
> tionary training for the proletarian uprising. What is the Bolshevisation of
> Communist Parties? It is giving them such a training, and effecting such a

selection of the leading staff, as would prevent them from drifting when the hour for their October strikes. 'That is the whole of Hegel, and the wisdom of books and the meaning of all philosophy...' [75]

Conclusion: the long view

Bourgeois ideology, as we noted in the opening section of this article, oscillates between idealist voluntarism, which rejects the determining role of material conditions and social relations, and mechanical materialism which sees human beings as passive objects and denies the role of conscious human practice. Both these modes of thought are generalisations arising from contradictory aspects of the social being of the bourgeoise and the social nature of capitalism. Idealist voluntarism reflects the position of the bourgeoisie as a ruling class, living off the labours of others, which imagines that its ideas and its will are the demiurge of history. Mechanical materialism reflects the subordination of the bourgeoisie itself to the economic laws of capitalism and its view of the working masses as mere factors of production.

Marxism rejects both these positions by taking as its starting point the social being of the working class. The working class encounters directly and inescapably the determining effects of both physical nature, the weight of the stone, the resistance of the metal, the cold of the winter, the heat of the sun, and of economic and social relations, the pressure of poverty, the necessity to sell its labour power, the impact of unemployment, the invisible but real obstacles to social mobility. Yet, at the same time, the working class is continuously and directly involved in the conscious effort to transform both nature and social relations. Potentially it has the collective power to overturn the entire social system and establish a new society in which it will simultaneously produce and consciously direct production. It is on this foundation that Marxism transcends idealism and mechanical materialism in dialectical materialism which finds its highest expression in conscious revolutionary practice. Conscious revolutionary practice is activity which makes use of the fullest possible understanding of all the natural and social forces constraining and shaping human behaviour in order to tip the balance in favour of the working class and rescue humanity from the abyss.

In every historical situation there is a tension between necessity and freedom, between what is objectively determined and what we can affect or change, but the balance between necessity and freedom is not fixed or stable. At the dawn of human history and for a long time thereafter the element of necessity was heavily dominant. Human behaviour was massively dominated by forces beyond our control, by the interaction between external nature and our own physical constitution. Yet also present from the beginning—indeed it is what marks the beginning—is the embryo of human freedom, namely conscious social labour. The whole of history is the struggle to expand human freedom through the development of the power of human labour.[76]

However this development has not been smooth or harmonious. It has proceeded dialectically, which is to say through contradictions. The raising of the productivity of social labour involved the division of society into antagonistic classes and the subordination of the labour of the majority to the direction and exploitation of a small minority. This process comes to a head under capitalism which leads to an unprecedented development of the productive forces and, therewith, mastery over nature, yet subjects the entire globe, including and especially the capitalist class itself, to the impersonal and inhuman laws of the market, the first of which is accumulation for accumulation's sake.

The socialist revolution is this resolution of this contradiction. It is, in Engels' phrase, 'humanity's leap from the realm of necessity to the realm of freedom'.[77] The realm of necessity is not, of course, abolished. Natural laws and forces continue to operate on human beings and compel them to labour,[78] and in its first phase socialism is 'still stamped with the birth marks of the old society from whose womb it emerges'.[79] Nevertheless with the establishment of workers' power the balance between necessity and freedom begins to shift decisively in favour of freedom. With each step taken towards the international abolition of classes and the unification of humanity, human beings take increasing control of their own destiny. As material scarcity is progressively overcome, so the 'tyranny of economics' is ended. What was hitherto the 'ultimately determining factor' in history, namely the production of the necessities of human life, while not disappearing, will play an ever decreasing role in shaping human behaviour. A new society will be established in which 'the free development of each is the condition of the free development of all'.[80] At this point historical materialism, having achieved its goal, also reaches its limit.

Notes

1   F Engels, 'Speech at the Graveside of Karl Marx', Marx and Engels, *Selected Works*, Vol II (Moscow, 1962), p168.
2   K Marx and F Engels, *The Manifesto of the Communist Party* (Beijing, 1988), p50.
3   K Marx, cited in F Mëhring *Karl Marx* (London, 1966), pp207-8.
4   K Marx, *The Poverty of Philosophy*, cited in D McLellan, *The Thought of Karl Marx* (London, 1971), p38.
5   For a fuller analysis of Kautskyism, see J Molyneux, *What is the Real Marxist Tradition?* (London, 1985).
6   A Gramsci, *Selections from the Prison Notebooks* (London, 1971), p336.
7   C Guevara, *Guerilla Warfare* (New York, 1967).

8   See especially V I Lenin, *Left Wing Communism—an Infantile Disorder* (Peking, 1965).

9   See, for example, Y Gluckstein, *Mao's China* (London, 1957); N Harris, *The Mandate of Heaven* (London, 1978); T Cliff, 'Permanent Revolution', in *International Socialism* 61 (first series).

10 See P McGarr, 'Order out of Chaos', in *International Socialism* 48, especially pp140-142.

11 R Miliband, *Class Power and State Power* (London, 1983), p132.

12 K Marx, 'Theses on Feuerbach', Marx-Engels, *Selected Works*, Vol 2 (Moscow, 1962), p403.

13 A Gramsci, op cit, p336.

14 K Marx, 'Theses on Feuerbach,' op cit, p403.

15 An account of these developments, for the layperson such as myself, is provided by P McGarr, op cit. McGarr also discusses their implications for determinism and argues convincingly a) that chaos theory constitutes a real advance in our scientific understanding of the world; b) that it does not represent a 'threat' or 'problem' for genuine Marxism.

16 Ibid, p147.

17 A Gramsci, op cit, pp336-337.

18 L Trotsky, *My Life*, (New York, 1970), p224.

19 J F Lyotard, *The Postmodern Condition: A Report on Knowledge* (Mimosa and Manchester, 1984), pxxiii.

20 K Marx and F Engels, *The German Ideology* (London, 1985), p48.

21 Ibid, pp42 and 50.

22 Ibid, p42.

23 K Marx, *Preface to A Contribution to the Critique of Political Economy*, in D McLellan, *Karl Marx: Selected Writings* (Oxford, 1977), p389.

24 K Marx, cited in D McLellan, *The Thought of Karl Marx* (London, 1971), p38.

25 Ibid, p38.

26 K Marx and F Engels, *The Manifesto of the Communist Party* (Beijing, 1988), p36.

27 K Marx, *Preface,* in D McLellan, op cit, p389.

28 C Bettleheim, *Class Struggles in the USSR, 1917-23* (Hassocks, 1976), p62. For a critique of Bettleheim, see A Callinicos, 'Marxism, Stalinism and the USSR', *International Socialism* 5.

29 A Callinicos, *Marxism and Philosophy* (Oxford, 1983), p112. The main part of Alex's argument for this proposition is to be found in ibid, pp48-52.

30 Ibid, p51.

31 This concept of a 'reaction back' is taken from Engels to C Schmidt, October 27 1890, in Marx-Engels *Selected Works*, Vol II, op cit, p494, where it is used to describe the influence of the law on the economy.

32 In *The German Ideology* Marx famously asserted that 'this development of the productive forces...is an absolutely necessary practical premise because without it *want* is merely made general and with destitution the struggle for necessities and all the old filthy business would necessarily be reproduced', op cit, p56. Moreover both Trotsky and Cliff grounded their analysis for the degeneration of the Russian Revolution in this insight.

33 K Marx, *Capital,* Vol III (Moscow, 1966), p791, cited in A Callinicos, op cit, p50. Alex's attempt to defend the primacy of the relations of production by counterposing the 'mature' historical materialism of *Capital* to the 'crude' version of *The German Ideology* is not consistent. He tells us that 'Marx resolved this unclarity by introducing in *The Poverty of Philosophy* (1847) the concept of the relations of production' (p49) and that 'with the explicit formulation of the concept of relations of production...historical materialism can be said to be fully

constituted' (p51). Yet, as we have seen, *The Poverty of Philosophy* is committed to the primacy of the production forces. See footnote 22 above.

34   C Harman, 'From Feudalism to Capitalism', *International Socialism* 45, p82.
35   F Engels, 'Speech at the Graveside of Karl Marx,' in Marx-Engels *Selected Works* Vol II, op cit, p167.
36   K Marx, *Preface,* op cit.
37   F Engels to J Bloch, September 21-22, 1890 in Marx-Engels *Selected Works* Vol II, op cit, p488. For alternative formulations and elaborations of the same ideas see F Engels to C Schmidt, 5 August 1890, ibid pp486-88, F Engels to F Mehring, 14 July 1893, ibid pp496-501.
38   K Marx, *The Eighteenth Brumaire of Louis Bonaparte* (New York, 1968), p15.
39   L Trotsky, *The History of the Russian Revolution* (London, 1977), p18.
40   F Engels to C Schmidt 27 October 1890, op cit, p493.
41   Though there are still very definite limits to this autonomy. The Nazi state remained a capitalist state in that it presided over a capitalist economy, preserved capitalist relations of production and could not have been used to expropriate the capitilalist class.
42   This analysis of Marxism, in opposition to the Althusserian view of it as autonomous theory or science, is outlined more fully in J Molyneux, *What is the Real Marxist Tradition?* op cit. The development of Marxism in the years 1843-1848 was highly determined in that it could not have emerged in an earlier period before the development of capitalism had reached a degree of maturity and before the proletariat had at least begun to make its presence felt. But it cannot be seen as absolutely determined. Without the individual genius of Marx it might have taken considerably longer for scientific socialism to have received coherent formulation.
43   It might be argued that though this was true in Marx's day, when it was a case of work or starve, it ceases to be true in the context of a welfare state. However, it is clear that no capitalist society would or could allow benefits to rise to the point where more than a tiny minority of the working class would voluntarily choose not to work.
44   Marx's labour theory of value is that the value of a commodity is determined by the amount of socially necessary labour required for its production. The relation of price to value is complex but essentially the value of a commodity is a notional average around which its actual price fluctuates.
45   See K Marx, *Capital,* Vol III, op cit, Part III.
46   For the most impressive statement, defence and application of Marxist theory of crisis to contemporary capitalism, see C Harman, *Explaining the Crisis* (London, 1987).
47   See K Marx, *Capital,* Vol III, op cit, ch xiv.
48   Though not, of course, in every specific instance.
49   K Marx, *Capital,* Vol II, op cit, ch xiv.
50   G E M de Ste Croix, *The Class Struggle in the Ancient Greek World* (London, 1981), p51.
51   The key passages from his writings have been collected and published as L Trotsky, 'The interaction between booms, slumps and strikes', *International Socialism* 20.
52   Ibid, p135.
53   Ibid, p139.
54   Ibid, p142.
55   A Gramsci, op cit, p438.
56   For an account of this episode and Lenin's assessment of it, see T Cliff, *Lenin,* Vol 4 (London, 1979), ch 5 and ch 7.
57   L Trotsky, *The History of the Russian Revolution,* op cit, pp121-122.
58   K Marx and F Engels, *The Manifesto of the Communist Party,* op cit, p49.

59   Ibid, pp32-33.
60   Which has not of course prevented it. Most notably the Posadasist Tendency—a
      fragment of the Fourth International—combined the 'inevitability' of socialism
      with the 'inevitability' of imperialist war and concluded that the Soviet Union
      should launch a preemptive nuclear strike on the West, secure in the knowledge
      that socialism would 'inevitably' arise from the ashes.
61   L Trotsky, *The Struggle Against Fascism in Germany* (New York, 1971), p137.
62   V I Lenin, *Selected Works*, vol 6 (London, 1936), p297.
63   Ibid, pp230-232.
64   Ibid, pp334-335.
65   L Trotsky, *Diary in Exile* (London, 1958), p54. This is not a chance or offhand
      judgement. Trotsky made it on several occasions. See *The History of the Russian
      Revolution*, op cit, pp343-44, and his *Letter to Preobrazhensky*, cited in
      I Deutscher, *The Prophet Outcast* (Oxford, 1970), p241.
66   Ibid, p242.
67   Cited in ibid, p244.
68   Trotsky himself is by the far the strongest alternative candidate for this role but his
      status as a newcomer to the party would almost certainly have disbarred him. It
      should be remembered that this still counted against him six years later in 1923.
69   J Molyneux, *Leon Trotsky's Theory of Revolution* (Brighton, 1981), pp64-65.
70   For how Deutscher's passive fatalist Marxism led to his capitulation to Stalinism
      see T Cliff, 'The End of the Road: Deutscher's Capitulation to Stalinism', in
      T Cliff *Neither Washington nor Moscow* (London, 1982).
71   L Trotsky, 'The Lessons of October', in *The Challenge of the Left Opposition
      (1923-25)* (New York, 1975), p201. For a full account of the German disaster see
      C Harman, *The Lost Revolution: Germany 1918-23* (London, 1982).
72   This example seems to me to refute the argument of Ralph Miliband that
      individuals can have an important effect on 'generated' history but not on
      'transgenerational' history. See R Miliband, op cit, pp143-152.
73   T Cliff, *Russia—A Marxist Analysis* (London, n d), p128.
74   V I Lenin, *Left Wing Communism—An Infantile Disorder* (Moscow, 1968), p52.
75   L Trotsky, 'The Lessons of October', op cit, p256.
76   It is a terrible irony and mark of human alienation that the profoundly true and
      profoundly Marxist statement, 'Arbeit macht frei', adorned the gates of the Nazi
      death camps.
77   F Engels, *Anti-Dühring* (Peking, 1976), p367.
78   'Just as the savage must wrestle with nature to satisfy his wants, to maintain and
      reproduce life, so must civilised man, and he must do so in all social formations
      and under all possible modes of production.' K Marx, *Capital*, Vol III, op cit,
      p820.
79   K Marx, 'Critique of the Gotha Programme', Marx-Engels, *Selected Works,* Vol II,
      op cit, p23.
80   K Marx and F Engels, *The Manifesto of the Communist Party*, op cit.

News from nowhere?

A review of Asa Briggs, **The History of Broadcasting in the United Kingdom—Volume Five: Competition 1955-1974** *(Oxford University Press, 1995), £45*

STUART HOOD

This is the fifth volume of what is somewhat misleadingly called *The History of Broadcasting in the United Kingdom*. It is really that history as seen from within the BBC for, although a work that is painstakingly researched, it depends on the voluminous BBC archive and interviews with members and ex-members of the BBC staff. But official records and internal memoranda are not necessarily witnesses of truth; they are often rewritings of history designed precisely for the archives. More importantly, the history chronicles but does not look critically at the role of the BBC, its nature as an institution or its place in the social and class structure of Britain.

There is therefore no comment on the close relationship between the BBC and Whitehall or the BBC and the establishment. The history treats these links as natural and unproblematic. Thus in the period under review one chairman of the board of governors—who *are* in law the BBC—was an ex foreign office official. The director general, the BBC's chief executive, had been a military secretary to the wartime cabinet serving under this official. The next chairman was the ex-head of the civil service. Today, continuing this tradition, the chairman is brother-in-law of a Tory minister and his wife a lady-in-waiting to the queen. During the period covered by *The History* the members of the board of governors included a former under-secretary of state at the foreign office, an earl, the chairman of a multinational corporation and the ex-head of a public school. The national governor for Northern Ireland was an ex civil servant who had been in charge of Churchill's maproom during the war.

The members of the board of governors are chosen by the government of the day from the list of the 'great and good' which is kept in Whitehall; from it the members of quangos and royal commissions are routinely drawn. The men and women selected to govern the BBC are not in any sense representative but are appointed because they are 'safe hands' who will know what is expected of them. Their task is to see that the policies of the BBC reflect a consensus in politics, in the arts, in 'taste'—which is frequently defined as 'mainstream broadcasting. 'Mainstream broadcasting' has always excluded 'extremes'. This means that political opinions which fall outside the parliamentary spectrum have been denied a voice—or granted one only grudgingly. The parameters of the 'mainstream' define not only a political spectrum; the same criteria were applied in the period covered by *The History* to popular culture. Thus 'pop music' which many governors disliked intensely and others found uninteresting was not broadcast. The refusal to understand or give expression to the pop culture of the late 1950s and 1960s left the field open to the 'pirates' who broadcast from boats off the coast to a large young audience.

Given the background of the governors it is not surprising that they should have spent a whole meeting in 1957 discussing an article in the *American Saturday Evening Post* entitled 'Does England Need a Queen?' The author was Malcolm Muggeridge, the writer and journalist who was under contract to the BBC. He was considered to be a 'radical' but would become notorious as a moral crusader alongside Mary Whitehouse. His article was considered to have overstepped the mark and a couple of his programmes were cancelled as a mark of disapproval. In the same loyal spirit the governors decided that there was no need for 'one or two serious programmes in which the functions and circumstances of the monarchy would be expounded or argued'.

These are relatively trivial matters and important chiefly as indicating attitudes. More important is that people of this class and social background were in charge of the BBC when there was a proposal to make a programme about the H-bomb. Recent research has shown that the Tory government of the day got wind of the project which was sabotaged after confidential exchanges at a high level on both sides. What is significant is that there is no mention in *The History* of the episode and its mainly off-the-record conversations and decisions. What alarmed the government was that the programme proposed to discuss the effects of the bomb on the civilian population, which it did not wish to alarm. It was on these grounds that the chairman of the board of governors later forbade the screening of Peter Watkins' film *The War Game*, on the effects of an atomic attack. The reason given was that it was 'too horrifying for the medium of broadcasting' although (Briggs adds) it was to be made available to invited audiences, who presumably were made of sterner stuff than the ordinary viewer.

One important element missing from *The History* is any account of the part the BBC was expected to play in the event of an atomic war. There is no doubt that the BBC was (and no doubt still is) closely involved in the emergency plans for this (or any other national 'emergency'). Thus it is unquestionable that BBC engineers helped to plan the communications to and from the various bunkers where our rulers were to survive the catastrophe. No doubt BBC personnel would have been on hand there. The role of the BBC suggests that there is little danger of the BBC disappearing; the government needs it too badly to let it die.

Over Northern Ireland *The History* is congratulatory. In 1969 the chairman, who was then Lord Hill, sent 'a message of appreciation and confidence' to the BBC's chief executive there. The problem for the BBC was admittedly a difficult one. How does an organisation based on the idea of a consensus conduct itself where no consensus exists? The Unionists in particular complained vehemently at any news coverage of Republican affairs. The BBC in Belfast, as the chief executive there explained, 'cut out' parts of filmed or recorded interviews which included 'violently or offensively expressed opinion' and avoided inviting people liable to use inflammatory language to take part in live studio discussions.

This policy was in fact one of censorship which was compounded by protestations of ignorance. For example, when in August 1969 Catholics were burnt out of their homes in the Falls Road by Protestants, the BBC in Belfast claimed that they did not know who started the trouble and who carried it out. The result was that reports, as one BBC journalist confessed later, 'gave no indication of who these refugees were…the public was not to know…who was attacking whom.' There is no mention of this in *The History*. It also plays down the rumpus over a report from Belfast by Alan Whicker for the *Tonight* programme for which the BBC first apologised profusely and then blocked the remaining programmes in the series. The incident is mentioned only in a footnote to a passage in the text which admits that 'independent reporting…was made almost impossible because of Northern Irish sensibilities', ie Unionist sensibilities. In fact there was no coverage of the situation in Northern Ireland by 'outsiders' for the next five years.

By contrast a good deal of attention is paid by *The History* to the programme *The Question of Ulster*, which was conceived of as a panel of 'wise men' who would listen to evidence from 'expert witnesses' (who had to be 'uncontroversial') from the opposing sides in Northern Ireland. This programme was strongly resisted by the British government in the

shape of Maudling, the home secretary, who had complained about interviews with members of the IRA, and by Faulkner, the Unionist prime
minister of Northern Ireland, who had complained about an item on the
activities of the Ulster Volunteer Force which he described as 'mischie-
vous.' The programme did, however, go ahead. Among the panel of
witnesses were Gerry Fitt, Ian Paisley, Bernadette Devlin, two members
of the Dail and a Unionist MP who agreed to take part although Faulkner
had set his face against the programme. In the event the programme was
seen, as Briggs records, by 7.5 million viewers, the majority of them in
favour of the exercise.

The whole episode is interesting because of the panic among the BBC
governors during the run up to the broadcast, the pressures from the governments in London and Belfast, the campaign against the idea by the
Tory press and the fact that it happened at all. What it illustrates is a deep
contradiction in the BBC. It is on the one hand an institution involved
with the establishment and the subject of overt and covert pressure from
government, and on the other it has—as its charter says—a duty to
inform.

The history of the BBC, going back to its earliest days, reveals the tug
between this duty, which many journalists and programme makers take at
its face value, and the pressure from the governors not to rock the boat. In
short there is a clash between what one might call the professional ideology of some of the staff and the wider ideology which the governors
personify and perpetuate. One executive in Northern Ireland—significantly he had been responsible, from London, for the idea of a debate on
the Irish question—put the situation there very clearly. The BBC was
expected, he observed, to stand by the government 'in the national
interest'. But which government? he asked—Westminster or Stormont?
There was a need for the media to function as the 'fourth estate', distinct
from the executive, the legislature and the judiciary. 'It must be left to the
media', he argued, 'to decide (within the limits of responsibility) as to
what to publish'. The parenthesis about responsibility is significant but it
was an important formulation from someone who was later to become the
butt of Thatcher's ire for suggesting at the time of the Falklands War that
Argentina had a case.

The concept of the fourth estate naturally raises the question of the
ideology that underlies news and current affairs reporting and the
validity of the claim to 'objectivity'. But the tension between the ideology of the professionals (another term that would require analysis) and
what one might call the institutional ideology has from time to time been
fruitfully exploited not only in journalism but in other areas as well.
Indeed it can be argued that during the period covered by this volume of
The History—the period that saw Greene as director general—the

exploitation of the contradiction has born fruit in various fields. This was the era that saw David Mercer pursue his anti-Stalinist politics in a series of TV dramas, the documentary realism of *Cathy Come Home* dealing with the housing crisis, the so called kitchen dramas sponsored by Sidney Newman who said, 'I am proud that I played some part in the recognition that the working man was a fit subject for drama and not just a comic foil in middle-class manners.'

One programme which is generally taken as an icon of the period is *That Was the Week that Was*, the hallmark of which was a lack of respect for some sacred cows in British society. It took politicians, the Church and the royal family as the butts of its jokes. But Macmillan, the then prime minister, had the measure of the programme and advised the postmaster general not to take any action about it because 'it is a good thing to be laughed over. It is better than to be ignored.' In fact the political thrust of the programme was similar to that of *Private Eye*, which some of those involved in the programme went on to contribute to. That is to say, it was the politics of the insider cocking a snook at figures of authority and was in no serious sense of the word a political programme that challenged the ground rules of society or made any coherent attack on its inherent injustices. What it did do was to strike a chord of disrespect in the British public—the audience at its peak was 12 million.

TW3 was described by a Conservative Party official as being 'extremely left wing, socialist and pacifist'. It did much to implant the idea in both the Tory party and the Labour front bench that the BBC was a nest of radicals. Such radicalism as there was, however, was 'professional radicalism' often fuelled by the experiences of men and women who saw at first hand the evasions, the dishonesty, the two faced nature of political spokesmen. The more truly radical currents within broadcasting were to be found in the Free Communications Group which included men and women not only from broadcasting but also from the press. The FCG's stated aims were the social ownership of the means of communication. This would require a 'radical change in the present state of society'. A beginning should be made by fighting for 'a change in the relationships between the state and workers in the industry and the community.' There were, Briggs darkly suggests, Marxist undercurrents of thinking in the FCG's spasmodic publication *Open Secret* which published what was often confidential information from inside the media institutions.

The FCG was deeply divided and in due course ceased to exist. What is not unconnected with this leftist current is the fact that the BBC faced in 1969 the first official strike in the history of the Association of Broadcasting Staff about pay and the effects of the government's incomes control system.

The question that *The History* poses implicity but does not attempt to answer is, how was the Greene era in the BBC possible? The answer is to be found in part in the economic situation of the BBC, which because of the rising graph of TV licences enjoyed a parallel rise in its income. This meant that it did not have to go to the government to ask for an increase in the licence fee—an approach which governments have exploited to put pressure on the BBC to behave properly.

The BBC was a beneficiary of the 'you have never had it so good' period under Macmillan. At a moment of prosperity and against a background of social changes, the cracks in the monolith could be and were exploited by broadcasters.

Things have become more difficult in recent times with the application of Thatcherite policies. These had clear aims. One was to ensure that the board of governors was in right wing hands. This was accomplished by appointments to the board who proceeded to support a policy of marketing in programme production which has a parallel in the NHS market system. Another was to destroy what Thatcher saw as the last bastion of trade union power—the broadcasting industry. This was accomplished by the stipulation that 25 percent of BBC production must be out of house. The result has been to casualise much of the television industry, to undermine working practices and wage levels. These developments fall outside the period covered by *The History*.

The work has considerable shortcomings but will be useful for anyone who wants to pursue research into the period. Tucked away in the footnotes are important clues for anyone with a good political nose.

Communism in the heart of the beast

A review of Michael E Brown, Randy Martin, Frank Rosengarten and George Snedeker (eds), **New Studies in the Politics and Culture of US Communism** *(Monthly Review Press, 1993), £12.99*

LEE SUSTAR

When the Communist Party USA (CPUSA) marked its 75th anniversary last October the event was hardly noticed.

But it was not always so easy to dismiss the CPUSA. The history of the CPUSA exposes the lie that American workers will never fight for socialist politics and organisation. After a difficult beginning in 1919 that saw two rival Communist Parties (CPs) form too late to influence a massive strike wave, the party managed to build in key sectors of US labour. But the in-fighting of the early years persisted, and soon became caught up the faction fight waged by Stalin for control of the Russian Communist Party and the Communist International (Comintern).

By the time of the stockmarket crash of October 1929, a thoroughly Stalinised CPUSA had expelled the Left (Trotskyist) and Right (Bukharinist) Oppositions and embarked on Stalin's ultra-left 'Third Period' policy. According to this line, the revolution was imminent; reformist political leaders and trade union officials were 'social fascists', the equivalent of Nazis. Membership stood at 7,000—smaller than either of the two parties that had formed in 1919.

Yet despite the excesses of the 'Third Period' the CP connected with, and helped to lead, an upturn in working class struggle that began in 1934. A split in the American Federation of Labour in 1935 formed the Congress of Industrial Organizations (CIO) to organise unskilled mass production workers. This coincided with the new Popular Front line from Moscow, which aimed to convince Western governments to ally with Russia against Nazi Germany. Yesterday's 'social fascists'—not just labour leaders, but bourgeois politicians like Democrat President Franklin Roosevelt—were now allies. By the late 1930s membership reached 75,000.

The CP was relatively isolated during the Hitler-Stalin pact of 1939-1941, but a renewed patriotic Popular Front policy during the Second World War saw membership rise to 100,000. The class composition of the party had changed.[1] Industrial workers were a declining percentage of membership, overwhelmed by an influx of professionals, labour bureaucrats and, most famously, Hollywood film scriptwriters and actors.

In the Cold War of the 1950s the party was repressed as the domestic agent of the US's rival, the USSR. But repression did not destroy the party—despite the jailing of several key party leaders and the execution of two CP members, Julius and Ethel Rosenburg. Rather the party, still numbering 25,000, virtually collapsed following the ideological crisis of Stalinism after the Russian invasion of Hungary in 1956.[2] Its hegemony on the US left had ended not because of the McCarthyite witch hunts, but because of its own politics.

Decades after it was effectively marginalised, the CP's legacy remains hotly disputed on the academic left. This is a debate which goes to the heart of the question of building for socialism in the USA today.

One one side are the 'orthodox' Cold War liberal historians, led by ex-CP journalist Theodore Draper, who argue that the CP was from the outset an alien force on the US left.[3] On the other side of the debate are New Left academics with social and cultural histories of CP work in the mass movements of the 1930s. Their aim is not only to provide a corrective to Draper's supposedly distorting focus on CP leadership, but to find inspiration and strategies for a revival of the US left. While acknowledging the twists and turns of Stalin's dictates, they stress continuities in CP activities as the organisation developed roots in mass movements.[4]

Whatever the considerable merits of the new historians' work, most have stumbled over what the CP's Popular Front 'success' meant in class terms. The CP's Popular Front and Second World War policy were retreats from—and even betrayals of—the earlier struggles which initially won the party its following in the labour movement and anti-racist struggles. Maurice Isserman denies this in his work on the CP during the Second World War, when he claims that the CP's enthusiastic strike-breaking did not 'lead to any general flight of working class members out of the party' and that the opposition to the wartime black struggle for jobs did not impede recruitment among blacks.[5] Indeed, Isserman has gone on to argue that the 'success' of the Popular Front makes the case for the left to support President Bill Clinton today.[6] Thus the debate on the legacy of the CP is, unavoidably, a debate on the potential for building a socialist alternative in the US in the 1990s.

The editors of the anthology *New Studies in the Politics and Culture of US Communism* want to further the debate precisely because of its currency: 'Think of the gross inequalities of class, race and gender in this country... These are among the issues which the CPUSA has placed at the top of its agenda for the past seventy years.'[7]

This collection of new CP historians and others is a strong challenge to the liberal anti-Communist historians of the CP. But the usefulness of the book is that it highlights a much more important debate within the US left over the CP. This can be summed up in three areas: Was the Popular Front proof of socialism's potential mass appeal or an exercise in class collaboration? Was the CP principled in fighting the oppression of blacks and women? Did the CP fight for the interests of rank and file workers in the labour movement?

The answers to these questions are not just quibbles over the historical record. They have everything to do with the prospects for socialists in the 1990s and the potential of the US working class to emancipate itself.

The Popular Front

Editor Michael Brown begins *New Studies* by challenging Draper's claim that the CP was from birth an alien force in US politics. Brown cannot deny that after 1928 the CP leadership faithfully executed every twist and turn of the Moscow line but he does not look at the CP's pre-Stalinist years to challenge Draper. Instead he looks to grassroots CP members for evidence of the organic relationship to the US working class.[8] By failing to challenge Draper's argument that the CP was born with an original sin of being pro-Moscow, Brown (and other new historians) fail to come to grips with the counter-revolutionary nature of Stalinism. The CPUSA was from the outset more dependent on Moscow than most Western CPs. It took Moscow's intervention to unify the two original CPs, and party leaders often relied on the Comintern to settle internal debates. But there is a qualitative difference between the weak and factionalised—but still revolutionary—CP of the 1920s and the rigid, authoritarian CP of the 1930s and beyond.

Mark Naison's essay on the Popular Front makes this clear. Arguing that the CP grew massively in the early and mid-1930s because of its involvement in a revived working class struggle, Naison shows how the Popular Front from 1936 served to undermine those struggles as the CP pursued an accommodation with top labour leaders and pushed for support for the Democratic Party. In 1936 the CP was key in preventing the labour and farmer-labour parties in various states from coalescing in a national labour party. Although CP leader Earl Browder ran for president, the party worked to ensure Roosevelt's re-election, 'thereby becoming the first party in US history to use a presidential campaign largely to assure the victory of one of its opponents!'[9]

When Roosevelt moved right to adapt to a more conservative Congress after 1938, Naison shows that the CP moved to the right with him, dropping socialist propaganda for the sake of 'unity of progressive forces.' What had began as a directive from Moscow to support the 'democratic bourgeoisie' took on a dynamic of its own as the party liquidated its shopfloor newspapers, recruited middle class liberals and took on an 'atmosphere of pragmatism'.

In other words, it was not the 'alien' character of the CP that undercut its effectiveness, but the changes in the party's class basis during the Popular Front period. Naison sums up:

> Some Popular Front causes had indigenous political roots. The movement for black equality, the organisation of industrial unions, even the vision of a multi-ethnic United States proud of its varied cultural heritage, represented the long repressed impulses flowering within a left milieu, not Soviet dictates being implemented on US soil. But the insistence on linking these democratic currents to a brutal Stalinist dictatorship as high-handed in its decision making as Ford or General Motors, exposed the Popular Front left to charges of hypocrisy and political cynicism... A strategy that unleashed powerful forces in behalf of worker and minority rights, it rested on the most fragile and vulnerable political foundations.[10]

Was there a genuine socialist alternative to the Popular Front debacle? John Gerassi's article on 'The Comintern, the Fronts and the CPUSA' serves as the anthology's left wing critique of the party. Unfortunately Gerassi rejects not only the cross-class Popular Front alliance, but also the policy of the working class United Front developed by the Comintern in Lenin's time. He argues that the United Front of workers' organisations advocated by Trotsky as the way to stop Hitler's rise in Germany would have inevitably failed. Instead, Gerassi favours the sectarian Third Period line and dismisses Trotsky's efforts to win ordinary CP members to a principled revolutionary policy.

Trotsky rejected such ultra-left posturing. Even after the Stalinists' first attempt at assassinating him, he argued that, whatever the crimes of the Kremlin and the betrayals of Western CP leaderships, rank and file Communists were sincere revolutionaries who could be won to genuine socialist politics.[11]

These ordinary CP members, ignored by the orthodox liberal historians, are the subject of the anthology's writings on the CP's impact on culture in the US during the 1930s. Annette Rubenstein, a former CP member, recalls how working class party activists were involved in a wide range of cultural activities, especially theatre. Newly politicised workers were an eager audience and were often actors and stagehands in plays in union halls and ethnic clubs. The concentration of CP members in the theatre centre of New York meant the workers' theatre influenced Broadway via the government funded Federal Theatre, which had 200 production units in 12 states, including at least 12 black companies. With a weekly audience of 400,000, Rubenstein estimates that an incredible one third of the population attended these productions from 1935 to 1939, when anti-Communists in Congress killed its funding.[12]

The theatre had to compete for its audience with Hollywood. Rubenstein argues that theatre's success in the 1930s was because the essential element of conflict in any play resonated with millions of workers who became conscious that their own daily struggles determined their fate:

> Together with the exhilaration generated by this activity itself, there was also the fact of frequent, if not continual, small victories. We could actually unionise a shop, lead a group to sit in at the welfare office until they were given the benefits they were entitled to, force a restaurant to serve a black customer... There were enough of these successful actions in our own immediate consciousness, often as the result of our own personal participation, to make us know that victories were possible.[13]

In other words, ordinary CP members' activity in struggle shaped the party's impact on culture far more than the stultifying Moscow line of 'socialist realism'. Alan Wald develops this argument in his essay on Communist Party writers: 'The meaning of the Communist experience is less a matter of literary form or content than of commitment to racial equality, anti-fascism, anti-capitalism, national independence of colonies, and similar values'—although these views were greatly distorted by Stalinism.[14] He shows that the CP's influence on writers did not end with the departure of 'big names' such as Granville Hicks over the Hitler-Stalin pact; fully seven eighths of the membership of the CP sponsored League of American Writers remained in the party.

While we know a great deal about the CP associations of black writers like Langston Hughes, Richard Wright and Ralph Ellison, Wald points out that dozens of writers who have received favourable critical attention like J O Killens and Chester Himes were also influenced by the CP. Many writers themselves denied past CP links because of changed political views or repression, and the literary establishment ignored them in order to keep ordinary people from a 'genuine history of their own cultural activities' and deny access to authors who wrote about workers' collective struggles and personal experiences.[15]

Wald shows that CP authors and poets were not just socialist realist propagandists. They turned out everything from epic poetry to pulp fiction during and after their years in the party. Women writers who were well known in the 1930s have since been ignored, including Christina Stead, Ruth McKenney, Grace Lumpkin and Dorothy Myra Page. Where the 1960s black movement was able to open up a mass audience for novelists such as Alice Walker and Toni Morrison, the 1950s witch hunts cut off literally hundreds of deserving CP writers from any critical attention whatsoever. Wald concludes that the literature of the 1930s will get the attention it deserves when a revived working class movement discovers its own history in order to fight for its future.[16]

Marvin Gettleman's essay on the CP's New York Workers School goes so far as to argue that the CPUSA leaders were unconscious Gramscians, trading in armed revolutionary struggle for 'contests for cultural hegemony'.[17] In fact his essay shows that what began as an important vehicle for educating trade union and socialist militants degenerated into a prowar propaganda vehicle. Whatever Gramsci meant by cultural hegemony, studying wartime Stalinist tracts on the need for unity not only with Democrats but also with Republicans was clearly not it.[18]

Fighting oppression

The CP's record in fighting the oppression of blacks and women has long been a focus for debate on the US left. Feminists in the 1960s and 1970s rejected socialism precisely because of the status of women in the so called 'socialist' countries and the CP's conservative pro-family line. Rosalynn Baxandall's article makes some concessions to feminism, but she does show that, despite the CP's awful position on women's oppression, the party went much further than any previous feminist organisation on the US left in politicising working class women and drawing them into struggles to fight for their own interests. Baxandall quotes writer Tillie Olsen: 'The CP took me out of a life of drudgery and into a life of action.' Women's membership in the party soared from 10 percent in 1930 to 50 percent in 1943 as the CP moved beyond the workplace to intervene in struggles against mortgage foreclosures, evictions, welfare, emergency food relief and more. Yet the CP newspaper *Working Woman* usually resembled publications aimed at middle class housewives. And the CP did nothing to protest when hundreds of thousands of women were forced from their wartime jobs and day care centres were closed at the end of the Second World War. The class collaborationist politics of the Popular Front required the abandoning of the struggle against women's oppression. One effort by a woman comrade in 1935 to open a debate on women's liberation led to her vilification and expulsion.[19]

Baxandall shows the inconsistencies in the CP's fight against oppression. Gerald Horne seeks to defend the record. His account of the election of black CP leader Ben Davis to the New York City Council is a challenge to historians Mark Naison and Robin Kelley, whose respective books on Harlem and Alabama show how the Popular Front alliance with the Democratic Party undermined the fight against racism. Horne reports that during the Second World War 'the membership of the Harlem party, and of black Communists generally, dramatically increased' with 500 recruited in the spring of 1943 alone. Davis was elected with a majority of black and nearly half of white first choice votes in a proportional representation election. His other evidence of widespread black backing for the CP was Davis's support from singer Lena Horne and boxer Joe Louis.[20]

The problem with Horne's argument is that, while the number of black recruits may have increased in the 1940s, the basis on which they joined had qualitatively changed. In the early and mid-1930s the CP increased party membership in Harlem from a handful to over 2,000 by engaging in fights against police brutality, the campaign against the racist frame up trial of the Scottsboro Boys and job discrimination and unemployment. In Alabama the party won black support by braving intense repression to build unions and fight for civil rights. In both cases the turn to the Popular Front alliance with Democrats compromised the principled fight against racism and led to the resignation of key black cadre. With the Democratic Party dependent on a racist one party state in the segregated South, there was no way the CP could support Democrat President Roosevelt and carry out a principled fight against racism.[21]

During the Second World War the CP could gloss over this contradiction as Roosevelt's order to desegregate the military seemed to hold out promise for a better post-war life for blacks. In fact, the significance of Davis's victory was seen not so much as a blow against racism, but as a step on the way of the CP's drive to get into the political mainstream. Gil Green, a top CP leader, said of the victory, 'If correctly appraised and followed up it may well mark the turning point of our party to the main forces in American political life—the beginning of full integration of our party into the camp of national unity...'[22]

Davis's victory was not a continuation of the CP's workplace and civil rights struggles against fighting racism, but a retreat from such militancy into electoralism and support for the Democratic Party. To be sure, the election of a black Communist caused a stir in local and US politics.

But in reality the Davis victory consolidated the CP's turn to electoralism and set the stage for CP leader Earl Browder's decision to dissolve the party in 1944 and merge it into the left wing of the Democratic Party to support Roosevelt's re-election in 'the greatest electoral effort in [the CP's] history.'[23]

Horne contends that the Davis victory would have marked the beginning of the Civil Rights Movement but for anti-Communist repression by the state. But the CP's record on the 'black question' is much more complicated than that. Horne is right to argue that the CP's theory of self determination for the 'black belt' in the former slave states was scarcely relevant to the party's actual practice.[24] But however wrong the theory, it did raise questions about the centrality of the working class in the struggle for black liberation in the US.[25] In shrugging off these issues, Horne by default accepts the CP's own Popular Front criteria for success: not 'How can we build black and white unity in labour and civil rights struggles?', but 'How many votes can we get?' By removing the class content from the struggle against racism in the Second World War Popular Front, the CP ensured that it—and the tens of thousands who left the party—would tail the middle class leadership of the Civil Rights Movement.[26]

The CP in the labour movement

No one disputes that the CPUSA was instrumental in the labour struggles that led to the formation of the CIO. The debate is over the CP's relationship to the labour bureaucracy, its role in enforcing the no-strike pledge in the Second World War, and its inability to withstand the purges and witch hunts of the 1950s.

Unfortunately, Roger Keeran's article sidesteps these questions. Keeran does provide a useful summary of the dramatic growth of the CIO—from 2.6 million in 1934 to 7.3 million in 1938—and documents the key role of CP members in building the unions. By the Second World War the party controlled unions with 25 percent of the CIO's membership. But by 1954 this was gone, with 59 unions barring Communists from office, and 40 barring CP members completely. Keeran explains this enormous setback as almost exclusively a result of state repression and red baiting by the labour leaders.[27]

In fact the CPUSA's own record in the labour movement is one of tragedy and betrayal. A number of labour historians show that, although the CP attracted the best militant rank and filers in unions such as the United Auto Workers, the Popular Front period saw the party becoming an appendage of the trade union bureaucracy. In the Transport Workers Union (TWU) the CP dominated the leadership.[28]

Instead of maximising rank and file independence from the trade union bureaucracy, the CP actively sought to make workers more dependent on 'allies' among union tops. For example, in 1938 54 percent of the trade union delegates to the 1938 convention were trade union functionaries, and 128 of 776 delegates were full time trade union officials.[29] Yet many of these union leaders denied CP membership—and only 27,000 of 75,000 party members were trade unionists.[30]

The CP's orientation on the union bureaucracy had a political impact, just as the CP's support for Roosevelt reinforced labour leaders' ties to the Democrats, with the exception of the period of the 1939-1941 Hitler-Stalin pact. The results were disastrous for the fight against racism in the working class. The greater the party's orientation to the union leadership, the less likely it was to take up the question of racism by the employers or within union ranks, especially as it supported the no-strike pledge during the Second World War.[31] What is more, the CP once again worked to short circuit the movement for a labour party during the war.[32]

With the Allied victory in 1945, employers, union leaders and the government expected struggle to resume—1946 saw the biggest wave of strikes in US history. But the working class had changed enormously since the sitdown strikes of the 1930s. The war economy had increased the size of the working class and the union membership as millions poured into the cities from rural areas. Even a revolutionary socialist party with roots in the working class would have faced a serious challenge in fighting for the leadership of such a massive strike movement, which the trade union bureaucracy intended to be a 'safety valve'. But the CP, with its middle class orientation, had no intention of doing so. Indeed, CP leaders initially called for the extension of the no-strike pledge, which put CIO bureaucrats considerably to the left of the CP.[33]

The result was political confusion and disorientation in the working class. Only 30 percent of trade unionists voted in the 1946 mid-term elections, which allowed the Republicans to take both houses of Congress (a feat unequalled until 1994). Anger with Democrat President Truman over his strikebreaking led to a split in the union leadership, with a labour party once again on the agenda. But with the onset of the Cold War, labour leaders went all out to mobilise unions to support Truman in the 1948 elections, while the CP supported a former Roosevelt vice-president in a weak third party bid. The next year the CIO expelled nine unions allegedly led by Communists (two others had already left) whose membership totalled nearly a million—between 17 and 20 percent of the total CIO membership.[34]

And so, at a time when the Labour Party won a massive victory in Britain and Canadian social democracy became a national force, the idea of a labour party in the US was stillborn because, as historian David

Brody put it, the CP had inhibited the growth of the labour left and the anti-Communism of the trade union bureaucracy 'burned out the roots of an independent labour politics'.[35] The CP could not withstand the pressure because for the previous decade it had oriented on the union leadership rather than sinking roots in the industrial rank and file. And having loyally supported the Democrats, it had no credibility when it broke with the labour bureaucrats who backed Truman in 1948.

All this led to defeat not just for the CP, but for the entire US workers' movement. The CIO leaders' anti-Communism drove out the anti-racist militants who would have been key to the 'Operation Dixie' Southern organised drive. But union leaders, worried about upsetting allies in the Democrats' 'Solid South', abandoned the drive—and the low unionisation rate in the South has undermined the US labour movement ever since.[36]

Conclusion

The decline of the Communist Party USA was not due to the supposed conservatism of US workers. Nor was the CP crushed by state repression, although articles by Stephen Leberstein and Ellen Shrecker show that the witch hunts were certainly pervasive and vicious.[37] Rather the party collapsed under the weight of its own Stalinist politics. The CP won credibility through the struggles and sacrifices of its membership— the best working class fighters of their generation. But all this was thrown away by policies which systematically subordinated the workers' movement to the trade union bureaucracy and the Democratic Party— the party that ran the US state in the 1930s and 1940s. Finally it was the disillusionment with Stalinism that led to the party's collapse.[38]

None of this was inevitable. The workers' movement internationally had the potential to defeat fascism and avoid the Second World War. But the small Trotskyist groups failed to break the stranglehold of Stalinism over the movement.[39]

Now the issues that led millions to join the Communist Parties around the world in the 1930s are back—attacks on trade unions, unemployment, hunger, war, and, most ominously, fascism. *New Studies in the Politics and Culture of US Communism* is a welcome contribution to the history of those struggles to aid a new generation to carry on the fight, finally free from Stalin's dead hand.

Notes

I would like to thank Lance Selfa and Pete Gillard for their suggestions for this review.

1   M Davis, *Prisoners of the American Dream* (London, 1986), p72.

2   M Isserman, *If I Had a Hammer...The Decline of the Old Left and the Birth of the New Left* (New York, 1987), pp3-34.

3   T Draper, *The Roots of American Communism* (Chicago, 1985 [1957]), p395. His second book, *American Communism and Soviet Russia* (New York, 1986 [1960]) covers the CP up until 1929. Another influential 'Cold War liberal' book is by another former CP journalist: J Starobin, *American Communism in Crisis, 1943-1957* (Berkeley, 1975). Draper's work—and interpretation—is developed in H Klehr, *The Heyday of American Communism: The Depression Decade* (New York, 1984).

4   The most important examples of this trend are: R Keeran, *The Communist Party and the Auto Workers' Unions* (New York, 1986 [1980]); M Isserman, *Which Side Were You On? The American Communist Party During the Second World War* (New York, 1982); M Naison, *Communists in Harlem During the Depression* (New York, 1983); R Kelley, *Hammer and Hoe: Alabama Communists During the Great Depression* (Chapel Hill and London, 1990); and F Ottanelli, *The Communist Party of the United States: From the Depression to World War II* (New Brunswick and London, 1991). Draper's reviews of these and other works in his 1985 afterword in *American Communism*, pp445-482, led to an increasingly bitter debate. See S Willentz, 'Red Herrings Revisited: Theodore Draper Blows His Cool', in *Voice Literary Supplement* (New York, June 1985), and T Draper, 'The Myth of the Communist Professors: The Class Struggle' in *The New Republic* (New York, 26 January 1987), pp29-36. Draper gave a hostile review of *New Studies* in 'The life of the Party', *The New York Review of Books* (New York, 13 January 1984).

5   M Isserman, op cit, pp164-169.

6   M Isserman and M Kazin, 'The Left and Clinton: As Bill Goes, So Do We', *The Nation* (New York, 30 May 1994).

7   Editors Preface, p9.

8   'The History of US Communism', in *New Studies*, op cit, pp15-34.

9   *New Studies*, op cit, p50.

10   Ibid, p69-70

11   For Trotsky's views on the Western CPs and an analysis of Western Communism in the post-war period, see C Bambery, 'The Decline of the Western Communist Parties', in *International Socialism* 49 (Winter 1990).

12   'The Cultural World of the Communist Party', in *New Studies*, op cit, pp248-255.

13   Ibid, p246.

14   A Wald, 'Culture and Commitment: US Communist Writers Reconsidered', in *New Studies*, op cit, pp285-286.

15   Ibid, pp284-285.

16   Ibid, pp295-301.

17   'The New York Workers' School, 1923-1944: Communist Education in American Society', in *New Studies*, op cit, p274.

18   'The consequences of [the] approach of an open mind, without prejudice, toward the Republican Party, will strengthen the forces of national unity within it and weaken the appeasement-isolationist-reactionary camp.' E Browder, *Victory and After* (New York, 1942), p122.

19   R Baxandall, 'The Question Seldom Asked: Women and the CPUSA' in *New Studies*, op cit, pp148-149; 156-157.

20   G Horne, 'The Red and the Black: The Communist Party and African Americans in Historical Perspective', in *New Studies*, op cit, pp213, 218.

21   M Naison, *Communists in Harlem*, op cit, pp114-165; 268-273, R Kelley, op cit, pp14-33; 131-135; 176-177.

22   Quoted in G Horne, op cit, p219.

23   M Isserman, *Which Side Were You On?*, pp167; 187-213.

24   G Horne, op cit, pp200-208.
25   For a revolutionary socialist critique of the CP's 'black belt thesis', see A Shawki,
     'Black Liberation and Socialism in the United States', *International Socialism* 47
     (Summer 1990), pp56-68.
26   T Branch, *Parting the Waters: America in the King Years, 1954-63* (New York,
     1988), pp210-212; 844-845.
27   R Keeran, 'The Communist Influence on American Labour', in *New Studies*, op
     cit, pp163-192.
28   B Cochran, *Labour and Communism* (Princeton, 1979), pp82-102; J Freeman, *In
     Transit: The Transport Workers Union in New York City, 1933-1966* (New York
     and Oxford, 1989), pp71-75.
29   'Report of Credentials Committee to the 10th National Convention of the
     Communist Party', 1938, *Browder Papers, Series II, Box 4, Folder 45, Tamiment
     Collection*, New York University.
30   F Ottanelli, op cit, pp152-157.
31   A Meier and E Rudwick, 'Communist Unions and the Black Community: The Case
     of the Transport Workers Union', in *Labour History* (Spring 1982), pp165-197.
32   N Lichtenstein, *Labour's War at Home: The CIO in World War II* (Cambridge and
     London, 1982), pp173-175.
33   M Davis, op cit, pp78-88.
34   Ibid, pp89-93.
35   D Brody, *Workers in Industrial America: Essays on the 20th Century Struggle*
     Second Edition (New York and Oxford, 1993), pp207-212.
36   M Honey, *Southern Labour and Black Civil Rights: Organizing Memphis Workers*
     (Urbana and Chicago, 1993), pp214-291.
37   'Purging the Profs:' 'The Rapp Coudert Committee in New York, 1940-42' and
     'McCarthyism and the Decline of American Communism', in *New Studies*, op cit,
     pp91-122 and 123-140, respectively.
38   A Stephanson, Interview with Gil Green, in *New Studies*, op cit, pp307-326.
39   See T Cliff, *Trotsky: The Darker the Night, the Brighter the Star* (London, 1994).

'To the teeth and forehead of our faults'[1]

PETER LINEBAUGH

A review of V A C Gatrell, **The Hanging Tree: Execution and the English People, 1770-1868** *(Oxford University Press, 1994), £20*

'The first law which it becomes a reformer to propose and support, at the approach of a period of great political change, is the abolition of the punishment of death,' stated Percy Shelley in his 'Essay on the Punishment of Death' (1813-1814).[2] Are we in such a period now? And does it therefore behove us to propose the abolition of the death penalty? To put the questions in perspective, if not to answer them, we may look at two revolutions of the past, the English Revolution and the Industrial Revolution.

To force money out of the City of London in 1640 Stafford advised Charles I to hang some recalcitrant aldermen. Two 'prentices were hanged instead, one tortured on the rack (the last time the instrument was used in England). The hangings hastened revolution.[3] Shelley understood the historical logic. Those who suffer for political crimes die,

> *...in such a manner to make death appear not evil but good. The death of what is called a traitor, that is, a person who, from whatever motive, would abolish the government of the day, is as often a triumphant exhibition of suffering virtue as the warning of a culprit.*

The conduct of Charles Stuart during his decapitation in 1649 did the royalist party more good than any other act of his reign. Thus, the English Revolution shows how the death penalty can help social change, and how it can stop it!

Turning to the Industrial Revolution, Shelley wrote about the death of another royal person, and sought to explain abolition of the death penalty and the Industrial Revolution. *We Pity the Plumage but Forget the Dying Bird: An Address to the People on the Death of the Princess Charlotte* was the title of his great abolitionist tract. Princess Charlotte died on 6 November 1817. At the same time Jeremiah Brandreth, Isaac Ludlam, and William Turner—the Pentridge rebels—were hanged and beheaded. They had led a wholly proletarian insurrection. Shelley unhesitatingly identified the evil 'in its simplest and most intelligible shape.' The 'day labourer gains no more now by working 16 hours a day than he gained before by working eight.' At the root of all: 'Many and various are the mischiefs flowing from oppression, but this is the representative of them all; namely, that one man is forced to labour for another...' How is the mischief of hanging 'represented' by forced labour? Gatrell, a Cambridge don, has written a big, thoughtful book about hanging during the period of the Industrial Revolution. So it is with great interest that we turn to it.

The book is in three parts. The first concerns the 18th century hanging crowd and the spectacle of plebeian culture. The second part concerns public opinion and the limits of sensibility. The third part concerns the resistance of the old order—the judges, the king and cabinet, or the hanging crew. The book is a major work of scholarship which will take its place with Foucault, Radzinowicz, Masur, Cooper and Potter.[4] Foucault downplays feeling, Gatrell writes. Radzinowicz is too Whiggish and 'distances us from repudiated parts of our history'. Materialist history ignores 'the inflation of new emotional repertoires'. Referring perhaps to Corrigan and Sayer, he writes that 'state formation is too blunt an instrument to serve our present purposes'.[5] What is Gatrell's approach?

Gatrell begins his book with the seminal jurist of the English bourgeoisie, Sir Edward Coke, writing in 1641. 'What a lamentable case it is to see so many Christian men and women strangled on that cursed tree of the gallows?' Gatrell comments rather too hastily, 'The order of the world depended on these slaughters,' without pausing to ask which order, or whose? Coke strove for quantification: 'insomuch, as if in a large field a man might see together all the Christians that, but in one year, throughout England, come to that untimely and ignominious death—if there were any spark of grace, or charity in him, it would make his heart to bleed for pity and compassion.' Gatrell's procedure is the reverse: the individual microcase arouses pity and compassion, rather than the large field or systematic study. The crux of his book derives from a statistical observation: a capital code consisting of hundreds of offences was suddenly reduced to a few during the 1830s, yet 'the noose was at its most active on the very eve of capital law repeals.'

Gatrell criticises 'Peel's easy way with figures' but Gatrell's are confused, scattered, and twice incomprehensible. 'There had been a mere 281 London hangings between 1701 and 1750', he writes on page 7 but then on page 8, quoting *The London Hanged*, he accepts that 1,232 people hanged at Tyburn in 1703 to 1772.[6] He does not attempt to reconcile these scarcely reconcilable statements. At another time he writes that '65 hanged in London between 1816 and 1830 as against 79 in the 80 years of 1701-80', another statement both careless and preposterous. This is not a book with quantitative interests. Who was hanged? How many were hanged? What were their crimes? What were the demographics: the social and economic background? Black people? Irish people? Gay people? Women? Men? Children? These questions are unanswered.

His study began with the chance discovery of the judges' reports and petitions for mercy regarding a rapist in Teakettle Row in Coalbrookdale, Shropshire, one of the classic sites of the Industrial Revolution and centre of the iron industry. In 1829 John Noden, a neighbouring wheelwright, raped Elizabeth Cureton, the daughter of an iron moulder. Gatrell tells a fascinating tale, while rigorously eschewing general propositions related to the violence of the mines or the mills, or of grown ups against children, or men upon women. Nor does he comment on wages, hours and profits, or how a person 'is forced to labour for another'. But we are astonished to learn that, in addition to the Noden case, 2,000 pardon petitions landed on Peel's desk in 1829.

'I discovered a mountain of appeals for mercy...unknown to historians.' 'Discoverers' of mountains find they had predecessors. This particular mountain was spied by Doug Hay 20 years ago.[7] Despite this Gatrell goes on to say, 'How deeply and on what levels the public scaffold permeated the English imagination in the century before its abolition has only lately been looked at.' When he says that the scaffold crowd has been 'all but excluded from historical study', it's difficult to agree, until, after reading similar remarks at the beginning of each chapter, one realises this is something of a writer's tic, associated with a tendency not to acknowledge others in the field, like Ronald Paulson, Doug Hay, Roy Palmer, John Beattie, to name a few.

The strengths appear on most every page: a forceful voice of narration committed to abolition, passionately realised microhistories, and the resources of thousands of 'humble' petitions with their occasionally cool or withering observations (a petitioner told Sir Robert Peel, 'A familiarity with scenes of blood has disqualified your august presence [from] rightly appreciating the life of man'). There is William Meredith MP, angry at the hanging of Mary Jones, her baby at her breast. There is the unsung radical James Harmer who broke the thief takers in 1816, who defended Bamford, and later the Cato Street conspirators. There is Sarah Lloyd, a servant girl hanged in 1800 for robbing her employer, supported by Capel Lofft (who once published an answer to Burke's *Reflections*) who stood with her on the scaffold denouncing the home secretary. There is Eliza Fenning asserting innocence to 45,000 at her hanging. Silvester did her. He, as recorder of London, was one in a line of hanging reprobates from Fleetwood, the malicious Elizabethan, to the notorious Stuart justice, Jefferys, who had held that office. 'Fallible magistrates', wrote William Hone in a tremendous pamphlet about the case, 'have grown old in the ministration of death.' There is Edward Harris who, despite an appeal dossier of 112 pages, was unable to make any speech as he intended, and could only vociferate 'innocent, murder!' Twelve hundred humble petitions a year arrived from 1812 to 1822, and twice that many afterwards. The voice of the common people in this evidence is 'the placatory capitulation of the hopelessly impotent'. Quivering with emotion, dealing with his own squeamishness, breaking taboos for the sake of history, Gatrell affirms that the gallows was a place of physical pain. Hanging was 'an offence against humanity'. 'The book is not only a history of emotions. It is also (in a measured sense I hope) an emotional book.'

Against these strengths are two major drawbacks. Firstly, its notion of 'the English people', to cite the subtitle, is a far cry from the people in England, and secondly, it does not examine these executions in relation to the production of value. These faults have the same root. They arise because, although Gatrell spends a lot of time with the hangers, he has little time for the hanged. There is no need to dwell on the strengths of the book—they are manifest—I wish to develop a debate. We may approach its drawbacks by referring to some notable omissions, the Romantic poets. Oddly they are not here, because the Romantics discover feelings and express them. They also opposed the death penalty. The Romantics raised an issue about class and hanging, and because Gatrell is tired of class he cannot deal with the Romantics—Shelley, Byron or Blake whose critiques of capitalism were root and branch.

Gatrell's expression is sometimes distorted by euphemism, jargon and vagueness. Thus society was marked by 'the increasing status differentiations of an economically dynamic, polarised, and urbanising society'. He cannot bring himself to write of capitalism. Instead he employs the common cliches of odious evasion. In the end, the scaffold spectacle will be repudiated 'by all manner of people lucky enough to swim with a rising economic or social tide'. Luck? Tide? Manner of people? This is writing which avoids analytical reasoning. Besides capitalism, he will not think in terms of class. At the end he confesses to being tired. The discovery of emotion 'left me with a diminished interest in how far *ancien régime* criminal law expressed class interests...' In this he says, 'I have not sought to comment on this debate directly, partly because it is now more than a little tired.' It is not the debate that is tired, but Gatrell. Listen to this yawn in a footnote in the middle of the book: 'We must take it as read here that throughout the 18th cent [sic!] and into the 19th, vast income inequalities, together with fluctuations in wages, work conditions, and food prices, and post-war unemployment, affected prosecution rates and the numbers hanged.' Why must this be taken as read? Where would it be read? What would we read? The full laziness of the stance emerges later.

Gatrell has stated what puts him to sleep. We may let him catch up on his rest. Meanwhile, Shelley, having raised the important question, provides us with the necessary jolt of caffeine. He was interested in those who tried to overthrow the most deadly regime in British history: the Irish workers of the 1790s, the expropriated people of Scotland, the vast numbers of enslaved producers of the plantations, the teeming multitudes, the *mobilitas vulgus* of the city, the machine breakers of the Midlands, and the artisans of the crafts provided an unstoppable entropy to capitalism. Yet they didn't quite yet form a 'class' in one well known Marxist schema. So it is unsurprising at the beginning of the period to find that Gatrell in the first part of his book describes the hanging crowds in the terminology of early modern Europe—the carnival, the plebeians. Edward Thompson wrote, 'A plebs is not, perhaps, a working class. The plebs may lack a consistency of self-definition, in consciousness; clarity of objectives; the structuring of class organisation'.[8] He argued that the plebeian culture was not a revolutionary culture: 'It bred riots but not rebellions: direct actions but not democratic organisations.' Its mode of action was symbolic or theatrical. Patricians and plebs performing 'theatre and countertheatre in each other's auditorium'. Gatrell advances the chronology of this theatre right through the Industrial Revolution, so that, despite the classic Marxist (and Thompsonian) narrative, there emerges no working class at all.

In an oxymoron Gatrell says that 'those who watched executions were far from uniformly lumpen.' He refers to 'the tatterdemalion poor'. He quotes the *Daily Telegraph* describing the crowd at the last public execution in England as 'a straggling motley procession...the beggars were coming to town...there was the wretched raggedness, there was the dirt, sloth, scurvy, and cretinism of rural vagabondage, trooping over the bridge.' The emphasis is on the rags (*lumpen* in German) which was picked up by Marx and Engels to make a powerful sociological category, the lumpenproletariat. Peter Stallybrass has shown how complex the term was; indeed, as the *Daily Telegraph* quote suggests, how *bourgeois* it was. He stresses two characteristics.[9] First, it conjoined depravity with racial fear. It was often perceived as foreign—*roués, maquereaus, literati, lazzaroni, la bohème*. Second, more looked at than looking, the lumpenproletariat was unsteady, protean, theatrical and clownish. The two characteristics are found in the two meanings to the term 'motley'. Even Marx in *Capital* refers to 'the motley crowd of labourers of all callings, ages, sexes', though Marx omits colour or ethnicity from his 'motley crowd'. When Thomas Dartmouth Rice opened with *Bone Squash Diavolo* at the Royal Surrey in London 1836 dressed in rags and singing 'Jim Crow' he got the jump on Marx by showing that poor people could represent themselves.[10] The black Atlantic people embraced scaffold wit nor did their consciousness deny its terror.[11]

Thompson found a more theatrical category in plebeian. As Marx and Engels sought a category of danger and volatility to contrast with proletariat, they found it in lumpenproletariat with its coloured theatricality. Gatrell makes use of both terms and he also writes with a pervasive sense of theatre. He compares the hanging crowd to the Greek chorus; he sees it peopled by 'stock' characters; he compares the hanging to a 'scene'; he describes the evidence of it as 'texts'; the emotional responses of those witnessing executions are called 'repertoires'. He refers to 'postures' in the culture of the urban *menu peuple*. Adopting an 1802 mouth filling term for an optical exhibition of imaginary figures who quickly change their size, he refers to the 'phantasmagoric array of characters' at hangings which at another point he calls 'an age old plebeian festival'. The danger of this writing is that it makes us spectators who watch history rather than actors who make history.

The process of expropriation had theatrical representations—this is true—but in itself it was a historical fact, not theatre: the gallows was as essential for the slave trade as for the punishment of vagabonds who had lost the commons. Stallybrass notes that Fanon figured *The Wretched of the Earth* and the lumpenproletariat in terms of the gallows tree of the coloniser. Oliver Goldsmith in 'The Deserted Village' (1770), the classic response of 18th century feeling to enclosures and the depopulation of the countryside, suggested that the gallows was one of the options in the limited choices available after enclosure:

> If to the city sped—What waits him there?
> To see the profusion that he must not share;
> To see ten thousand baneful arts combined
> To pamper luxury, and thin mankind;
> To see those joys the sons of pleasure know,
> Extorted from his fellow-creature's woe.

Here, while the courtier glitters in brocade,
There the pale artist plies his sickly trade;
Here, while the proud their long-drawn pomps display,
There the black gibbet glooms beside the way.

Gatrell's main source of information for his first section is the Francis Place collection which was gathered by the aging London radical by asking his friends to recollect the ballads of their youth. Thus the flash ballads became 'texts'. Gatrell is not the first to have noticed the demise of the older oral culture, and the suppression of ballads and chanting— Mayhew described and regretted it. Gatrell usefully explains how the huge, printed, pedagogical effort by Jemmy Catnach and Hannah More, the anti-radical Tory publicists, transformed a transgressive to a sentimental culture. He concludes:

> *It is foolish to look for uniform postures 'radical' or 'deferential' as the case may be. People steered a wavering course between tacitly ethical approval, sardonic and transgressive defiance, and mockery, sentimental anguish, or outright voyeurism.*

'People' perhaps did. People means many thousands of persons, tens of thousands of persons. Plebeian persons and otherwise. One of them was William Blake, who thought about this subject long and hard: deeply, magically, mythically and personally. The sheriffs closed Tyburn in 1783 after hanging the man to whom Blake had almost apprenticed himself years earlier. Why does Gatrell not bring up Blake as a scaffold witness? I'll explain by and by.

This is a middle class book, at least according to the author, it is for 'those of us who eat, prosper, and are safe.' Its meat and potatoes may be found in the middle in ten substantial chapters about 'how the middle classes felt about the bloody code, or the polite and would-be polite classes.' These are chapters about manners, religion, education, sensibility, evangelicalism and the utilitarians. The aesthetic repugnance of the fastidious and the squeamishness of the dainty increased the aversion to the 'bloody code' of 'the middle-to-middling classes'. Adam Smith and Francis Place said that the expansion of commerce and manufactures softened social relationships. Gatrell interprets a hanging dream that disturbed Charles Darwin. He explores and appreciates James Boswell's curiosity ('I was sure that human life was not machinery'). Contrasting them with the irony of the plebs, Gatrell calls these people merely facetious, because 'the killings were for or by them'. They had the neck for the job, but not the stomach. Gatrell is influenced by Peter Gay who, inspired by Freud's *Totem and Taboo*, considers civilisation a punishment upon a primal, prehistoric crime.[12] Yet the book is relatively free of

blather about 'Western societies' and its platitudes ('we know what a
fragile construct civility is') are mercifully few.

While students of British terrorism will be disappointed in not finding
the subject directly addressed—this was the period when Burke's doc-
trine of the sublime was adumbrated directly from his observations of
hangings—nevertheless the creation of dread in particular segments of
the labour market, or the production of anxiety at the social level, are
evidenced by numerous examples. Lord Chief Justice Ellenborough
wrote, 'Men are punished not with reference to the extent of their own
crimes, unless they be very great, but with reference to the number and
circumstances or similar cases committed by others at the same time.'
The same was said of women. The home secretary, Portland, denied
mercy to Sarah Lloyd in 1800 with the reminder that 'the great object of
punishment is example.' According to William Hone, Eliza Fenning was
hanged in 1815 to terrorise maidservants:

> All the masters and mistresses of families, whose credulity or idleness ren-
> dered them proper subjects for alarums, were excessively devoted to the
> vociferous execration of the wickedness of servants... Thus a general cry was
> raised for the hanging of Eliza Fenning, as an example to all maidservants
> suspected, upon presumption of murderous intentions.

Archdeacon Paley expressed the view most directly saying it was necessary for the innocent to suffer lest the guilty escape. 'What can we do
more than Pilate did under similar circumstances?' acidly asked John
and Leigh Hunt than 'wash our hands upon the *accident* of guilt or innocence and go to dinner?'

What did the lord chancellor look for in selecting a judge? Answered
one: 'A gentleman, and if he knows a little law so much the better.'
Sydney Smith tried to understand their justice. 'The principle is, because
a man is very wretched, there is not harm in making him a little more so.'
Or, 'To force an ignorant man into a court of justice, and to tell him that
the judge is his counsel, appears to us quite as foolish as to sit a hungry
man down to his meals, and to tell him that the table was his dinner.'
Gatrell savours the sarcasm against the 'sable bigots'. What will bring
them down?

At the end of his book he has this great sense of *discovery*, as he
reveals the *secrets* of power: 'We hide ourselves behind the arras,' he
says. Polonius, we recall, hid himself behind the arras in order to eaves-
drop on Hamlet while Gertrude, his mother, scolded him. Polonius made
a noise. Hamlet lunged at the arras with his sword, and Polonius was
slain—'Thou wretched, rash, intruding fool, farewell.' What was
Polonius doing there in the first place? He went there on behalf of

Claudius, Gertrude's husband, the king of Denmark, who had slain his own brother, Hamlet's father. Claudius suspects that Hamlet has discovered him. He sends Polonius to find out.

Gatrell thus wants us to assume the part of Polonius, and to be a spy. The last part of the book is about listening in on the secret meetings of the king in council, and the king would fall asleep, when they decided which among those sentenced by judges to be hanged would be granted a reprieve and which would not. This is a chapter to be relished. The increases of hangings in the 1820s was less the cause of the Old Bailey judges or those on the Assize circuit than of the king, the archbishop, the lord chief justice, the recorder of London, cabinet ministers and privy councillors meeting to determine who was to get mercy and who not. Although 'the king had recourse to laudanum' before the meetings, it is unclear whether his naps were caused by the narcotic or not. We savour the spying at a cost, however, on the grounds that history is made, not behind the arras, but in the streets and fields, as Byron described.

Gatrell enlists Byron as an innocent observer only to ignore Byron the ardent abolitionist. In February 1812, at the age of 27, Lord Byron, 'hot from the furnace of riot and near revolution in Nottingham', delivered his maiden speech in the House of Lords.[13] It was debating the bill which made the breaking of stocking frames a capital offence. The first major test over the conditions of acceptance of machines in the industrial revolution was being fought in the Midlands. Byron was there and reported 'several notorious delinquents had been detected—men, liable to conviction, on the clearest evidence of the capital crime of poverty; men, who had been nefariously guilty of lawfully begetting several children, whom, thanks to the times! they were unable to maintain.' He turned to the ruling class in the House of Lords:

It is the mob that labour in your fields and serve in your houses, that man your navy, and recruit your army—that have enabled you to defy all the world, and can also defy you when neglect and calamity have driven them to despair! You may call the people a mob; but do not forget that a mob too often speaks the sentiments of the people... Setting aside the palpable injustice and the certain inefficiency of the bill, are there not capital punishments sufficient in your statutes? Is there not blood enough upon your penal code, that more must be poured forth to ascend to heaven and testify against you? ... Will you erect a gibbet in every field, and hang up men like scarecrows? Or will you proceed (as you must to bring this measure into effect) by decimation?... Are these the remedies for a starving and desperate populace? Will the famished wretch who has braved your bayonets be appalled by your gibbets? When death is a relief, and the only relief it appears that you will afford him, will he be dragooned into tranquillity? Will that which could not be effected by your grenadiers be accomplished by your executioners?

Byron reports on an experienced working class, which in word and deed has already developed a critique of capitalism. It is a working class fully in the throes of thanatocracy (thanatos—Greek for death), and at the crux of industrialisation when the rate of surplus value advanced by lengthening the working day, or, when that met insuperable opposition, the rate increased by reducing the necessary value of the working class. 'What you gain in labour, I lose in substance,' as the worker says to the employer. 'Capital cares nothing for the length of life of labour-power', Marx wrote in *Capital*, published the year before public hangings came to an end. Overwork in the potteries led to the 'slow sacrifice of children'. In June 1863 all the London newspapers were filled with the sensational death of Mary Anne Walkley, age 20, who died of overwork whilst making dresses for the ladies attending the ball for the newly imported Princess of Wales. 'The capitalist mode of production...produces the premature exhaustion and death of labour-power itself. It extends the labourer's time of production during a given period by shortening his actual lifetime.' The struggle over the length of the working day Marx calls a protracted and dissembled civil war.[14] The death penalty is at the apex of this war, infrequently exercised, frequently imitated.

Gatrell does not see executions as part of thanatocracy, or the continuum with other forms of state sanctioned murder, or with other types of capitalist punishments. This was precisely Byron's and Shelley's theme. Moreover, they contemplated the utility of hanging to the corruption of the oppressed. Shelley wrote, 'Men...come to connect inseparably the idea of their own advantage with that of the death and torture of others.' Shelley argued that hangings helped to reduce the value of labour power:

The spectators who feel no abhorrence at a public execution, but rather a self-applauding superiority and a sense of gratified indignation, are surely excited to the most inauspicious emotions. The first reflection of such a one is the sense of his own internal and actual worth as preferable to that of the victim whom circumstances have led to destruction.

Hangings became functional to the creation of divisions within the working class—of race, ethnicity and nation.

Besides assiduously avoiding the analytical construct, as well as the historical reality, of capitalism, *The Hanging Tree* suffers mildly from nationalism. Gatrell sums up the significance of the repeal of the 'bloody code': 'It was as if England had become another and gentler country—or a little more like other countries.' Later an alarming note enters the tone:

Benjamin Ellis, a Waltham Forest labourer, was 'ascertained to be *too busy* with the deer and wood' and was transported, thus disappearing 'from English history'. Sarah Wharmby, a maidservant who stole her mistress's quilt, was also transported to Van Diemens Land and 'disappeared from English history too'. He indulges even in some ethnic rah rah—'Anglo Saxons needed these evasive defences rather peculiarly, it seems'—and some retro-Podsnappery—'A guillotine would do the killing better, if only that machine were not so French.'[15]

Otherwise his insularity is admitted, even proclaimed. Referring to mayhem in court, bias against prisoners, and the speed of trials, Gatrell imagines the conservative historian warning, 'Paint not the island story therefore, in darkest hues,' to which Gatrell replies:

> *You don't have to be a Marxist historian to see that what happened in the early 19th century courtroom takes us to the heart of the shadows. These things should not be left wholly off our island record.*

No, of course not. But why so defensive? Whence the accusation? Let us go back a moment. Before Hamlet killed Polonius, he spied upon Claudius who was trying to pray:

> *May one be pardon'd and retain th' offense?*
> *In the corrupted currents of this world*
> *Offense's gilded hand may shove by justice*
> *And oft 'tis seen the wicked prize itself*
> *Buys out the law. But 'tis not so above.*
> *There is no shuffling, there the action lies*
> *In his true nature, and we ourselves compell'd,*
> *Even to the teeth and forehead of our faults,*
> *To give in evidence.*

I propose that the offence in this case is national insularity. Further, I argue that the hangings cannot be pardoned without giving up the insularity, because hangings helped to constitute the imagined notion of England. Everything else is shuffling. We see Dickens shuffle. By 1849 Charles Dickens changed his mind and favoured the death penalty. He went to watch the hanging of Mr and Mrs Manning. She was a Belgian, and had shouted at her trial, 'There is no law or justice to be got here! Base and degraded England!' A few years later Dickens published his counter-revolutionary novel *A Tale of Two Cities* (1859) in whose first chapter Dickens summarizes the essence of the English and French nations by the personality, character and behaviour of their executioners. Religion, property, language, work, agriculture, industry—whatever

might be said to differentiate national characters—are here figured
entirely by the death penalty.

In 1973 when we were putting together our research at the University
of Warwick for a book on 18th century crime we chose a title, *Albion's
Fatal Tree*, from William Blake who is the third Romantic poet whom
Gatrell ignores. It is a symbolic title, with mysterious resonances, which
only now with the work of Ben Anderson and Jonathan Mee am I beginning to understand. Gatrell also chose 'tree' like us. Strictly speaking it is
a misnomer, because culprits did not hang from trees. There were parts
of the English speaking world where hangings *were* from trees. Indeed
Lord Baden-Powell called one such hanging place in Africa the
Christmas Tree. It is not just that deforestation was more widespread in
England, nor that a mechanical contrivance replaced a natural one. The
'hanging tree' had become a symbol laden with meanings. We see this in
William Blake writing in 1795:

> *The Tree still grows over the Void*
> *Enrooting itself all around*
> *An endless labyrinth of woe!*

> *Round the pale living Corse on the Tree*
> *Forty years flew the arrows of pestilence.*

His language of liberation is based upon a critique of Tyburn, 'Where
Satan the first victory won.' In Blake the fatal tree refers to the human
sacrifices alleged by Roman writers on the Druids. The relation of the
Druids to Rome and English history became a subject of antiquarian
interest in the 18th century with passionate disagreement about the
origins of the British state. When Blake took up this argument in the
1790s, it was parallel to the more celebrated debate between Burke and
Paine. Blake, like Old Hubert or Wordsworth ('It is the sacrificial altar
fed/With living men'), says that the Druids laid the foundations of the
British state. The Druids crushed the original liberty of an egalitarian,
bardic time.[16] 'Albion slept beneath the Fatal Tree.' Like Shelley to
whom abolition was the first law of political reform, for Blake the death
penalty's abolition was part of a general project for the realisation of
Jerusalem.

The gallows, like human sacrifice, played a part in the formation of
the nation, as an imagined community. Anderson suggests that executions form part of the nation's biography, and in some cases actually
constitute it.[17] Antique slaughters become family history, a kind of fratri-
cide took place, a blood compact. Tyburn elides the hangers and the
hanged, in 'bloody ole Englande'. 'The principle of the law was, that the

execution of a person was the act of the whole nation,' said the defenders of public execution. In employing the metaphor in *The Hanging Tree* Gatrell thus alludes to a Blakean argument that subverts his own chauvinism. It explains his mistakes. Gatrell writes that 'Scotland (and Ireland's) relative innocence of the noose continued into the mid-19th century'. Oh? Grattan said, 'The more you hang, the more you transport, the more you inflame, disturb, and disaffect.' He referred to the house burnings, pitch cappings, and half hangings of official lawlessness. The Wexford Rebellion of 1798 was sparked in May by the hanging of 28 prisoners at Dunlavin and a further 28 at Carnew.[18] The bridges across the Liffey were adorned with gallows of the summarily condemned in 1798. Having read Bob Scally's recent study of the Ballykilcline Rebellion of 1846, it is impossible to speak of 19th century innocence.[19] Gatrell wears historical blinders.

He won't see what he can't see. He examines a picture of the execution of the five Cato Street conspirators—'the detailing is lasciviously complete', he comments—however, the artist depicts every head but that belonging to William Davidson which is quite obscured by the executioner's shoulder. Davidson was descended from slaves. From the picture we would have no idea that he was a black man. That he was Jamaican is likewise hidden from Gatrell's commentary on the facsimile of his handwriting reproduced as an illustration. He refers to it as 'copybook aphorism in copybook script', but surely it looks different in the light of the experience of Jamaican Methodism: 'Thou shalt not oppress a stranger in a strange Land', or, 'thou shalt not pervert the judgement of a stranger', or, 'He that answereth a matter before he heareth it, it is folly and a shame upon him.'

When it comes to recounting or explaining the abolition of public hanging in 1868, the insularity becomes particularly obtuse, because extra-insular concerns were so prominent. For one thing it was an Irish Fenian who was the last person publicly hanged in England, at a high point in 'Fenian fever' affecting the British Isles, North America and the First International.[20] For another, it was the hanging in 1864 of the five pirates, four from Manilla and the fifth a Levantine, for a mutiny aboard the *Flowery Land* en route to Singapore. Lascars, as Asiatic sailors were called in England, arrived in England at the rate of 3,000 a year. They received one sixth of European pay.[21] Their hanging brought an enormous scaffold gathering described in full heterogeneity and more than 1,000 law enforcement officials. A costermonger, as reported to a parliamentary commission, said, 'So help me, Bill, ain't it fine; five of them and all darkies.' The crowd may not have been the international working class of proper aspiration, but its inchoate danger arose from the unpredictability of planetary workers. The reaction in the House of Commons was instantaneous: John Hibbert moved to abolish public executions.

'Was it merely a coincidence that just as the 1832 Reform Act presaged the end of gibbeting and anatomising and the repeal of the most capital statutes, so the Reform Act of 1867 presaged the end of public executions?' He is beguiled by the questions and never quite answers them, perhaps for the reason that they omit another 'coincidence'. The largest slave rebellion in Jamaican history, the Baptist War of 1831-1832, after which 232 were hanged, led to emancipation in 1833.[22] The end of public execution in England was presaged by the Jamaican Morant Bay Rebellion in 1865 led by Paul ('Cleave to the Black') Bogle after which 400 were flogged and 1,000 were hanged.[23] The labour moved by capital had neither an ethnic nor a territorial identity. These were moments of deep international class recomposition against which the narratives of the *English* franchise and *English* hanging need to be situated. 'There ain't no black in the union jack.'

Thus we take the argument 'even to the teeth and forehead of our faults'. We must, for it enables us to come to the present, and to note again Shelley's starting point. The judicial committee of the Privy Council, meeting on the first floor of Downing Street, remains the court of last resort for the British West Indies. Bermuda retains the death penalty; its governor is David Waddington QC, who delivered the call for a return to the death penalty at the Conservative Party conference in 1990. The government of Trinidad and Tobago flouted an undertaking with the Privy Council in 1994 and executed Glen Ashby, a mentally ill stonemason, by hanging him for two hours. It was the first execution in 15 years. The death row of St Catherine's Prison (formerly a slave market) in Jamaica contains more than 300 people, most of whom are kept in cages. Jamaica's minister of national security, K D Knight, announced in the summer of 1994 proposals to speed up executions. The last hanging was in 1988. He was responding directly to a group of businessmen who were protesting against the robbery and murder in May of a tourist at the resort town of Ocho Rios. Owing to crime the tourist trade had fallen to its lowest level in a decade. In Jamaica a direct correlation is thought thus to exist between the balance of payments and hanging, a view shared in the World Bank and the IMF.[24] In 1808 in London Samuel Romilly and Basil Montagu formed the Society for the Diffusion of Knowledge upon the Punishment of Death. That knowledge must include slavery or how one person is forced to work for another. The Anti-Slavery Society survives going on two centuries, and its work now is more daunting than ever with perhaps 100 million slaves on the planet today.

Notes

1   I thank my friend, Misha Jakobson, for helping me think.

2   D L Clark (ed), *Shelley's Prose, or The Trumpet of a Prophecy* (Albuquerque, 1954), pp154-158.

3   C Hibbert, *Charles I* (Harper & Row, 1968), p150.

4   M Foucault, *Discipline and Punish: The Birth of the Prison*, translated A Sheridan (Penguin, 1979), L Radzinowicz, *A History of English Criminal Law and Its Administration*, 4 vols (Stevens and Sous, 1948), D D Cooper, *The Lesson of the Scaffold: The Public Execution Controversy in Victorian England* (Ohio University Press, 1974), L P Masur, *Rites of Execution: Capital Punishment and the Transformation of American Culture, 1776-1865* (Oxford University Press, 1989), H Potter, *Hanging in Judgement: Religion and the Death Penalty in England from the Bloody Code to Abolition* (SCM Press, 1993).

5   P Corrigan and D Sayer, *The Great Arch: English State Formation as Cultural Revolution* (Blackwell, 1985).

6   P Linebaugh, *The London Hanged: Crime and Civil Society in the 18th Century* (Penguin, 1991).

7   D Hay et al, *Albion's Fatal Tree: Crime and Society in Eighteenth Century England* (Allen Lane, 1975), ch 1.

8   E P Thompson, *Customs in Common* (Merlin Press, 1991), p57.

9   P Stallybrass, 'Marx and Heterogeneity: Thinking the Lumpenproletariat', in *Representations* 31 (Summer 1990), p72.

10 W T Lhamon Jr, 'Performing the Lumpenproletariat: *Bone Squash* in London, 1836-37', in his forthcoming book *Raising Cain*.

11 P Gilroy, *The Black Atlantic: Modernity and Double Consciousness* (Harvard University Press, 1993).

12 P Gay, *The Cultivation of Hatred* (Fontana, 1993), vol 3 of *The Bourgeois Experience*, pp160, 181.

13 M Foot, *The Politics of Paradise: A Vindication of Byron*, (New York, 1988) p135.

14 K Marx, *Capital: A Critical Analysis of Production*, ed and translated Dona Torr (London, 1946), pp239ff.

15 Mrs Podsnap was a character in Charles Dickens' *Our Mutual Friend*. She exemplified British Philistinism.

16 J Mee, *Dangerous Enthusiasm: William Blake and the Culture of Radicalism in the 1790s* (Oxford University Press, 1992), ch 2 especially. A Liu, *Wordsworth: The Sense of History* (Standford University Press, 1989), pp190-198.

17 B Anderson, *Imagined Communities: Reflections on the Origin and Spread of Nationalism*, revised edition (Verso, 1991).

18 Grattan is quoted by J Smyth, *The Men of No Property: Irish Radicals and Popular Politics in the Late Eighteenth Century* (St Martin's, 1992), pp173-175, but see also B Henry, *The Dublin Hanged: Crime, Law Enforcement and Punishment in Late Eighteenth Century Dublin* (Irish Academic Press, 1994).

19 R J Scally, *The End of Hidden Ireland: Rebellion, Famine, and Emigration* (Oxford, 1995).

20 P B Ellis, *A History of the Irish Working Class* (Braziller, 1973), p140.

21 R Visram, *Ayahs, Lascars and Princes: Indians in Britain, 1700-1947* (Pluto Press, 1986), ch 3.

22 Daddy Samuel Sharpe told Rev Bleby, 'I would rather die upon yonder gallows than live in slavery.' He was the last British slave to be executed before emancipation. See P Fryer, *Black People in the British Empire: An Introduction* (Pluto Press, 1989), p95.

23 H Campbell, *Rasta and Resistance: From Marcus Garvey to Walter Rodney* (African World Press, 1987), p38.

24 *Times*, 16 July 1994, *Boston Globe*, 9 July 1994, *Toledo Blade*, 13 January 1995.

Back to the future

A review of Alex Callinicos, **Theories and Narratives: Reflections on the Philosophy of History** *(Polity Press, 1995), £12.95*

GEORGE PAIZIS

Their life and ours takes an exactly opposite direction. If we laugh, it's about what makes them turn pale. If they laugh, it's over something that we hate.
Robert Antelme

As capitalism ceaselessly strives to expand, drawing ever greater numbers of people more tightly into its web, so it becomes more unstable and increases the forces that can oppose it. As it looks forward towards the ever greater globalisation of production, so the competition between its constituent elements becomes more intense, so its own institutions act as a drag on the present. As the pace of change accelerates, so is the past brought to the present, and the present is seen more clearly in terms of its future consequences.

Callinicos's book about the nature of history is, therefore, very timely because we need to establish the difference between what Trotsky might have called 'their history and ours'. This book is a response to currents of thought making the academic rounds that challenge either historical materialism or the tradition from which it emerged. It is also a call to action in response to a more immediate need, because the debate surrounding history is gaining urgency and wider currency. The recent re-emergence of fascist organisation across Europe has made attacks on Holocaust revisionism more important and has drawn many more into the debate than ever before. Unwittingly, governments stir up debate whenever they seek legitimation. For example, the commemoration of

various events related to the Second World War certainly gave governments an opportunity to don cloaks of righteousness, but it also exposed
divisions between them. More importantly, it provided the opportunity
for people to measure their subsequent social and political experience
against what they had been told and not told at the time. Teachers,
parents and school governors were brought into the debate about historiography and the nature of history as the Tories searched for ways to
strengthen their control over the school curriculum. At the same time,
history is gradually becoming a part of the entertainment and culture
industry. This popularisation takes many forms—biopics, Vietnam or
recently-dead-president films from Hollywood, widely viewed serials
with computer assisted graphics like BBC2's *Storm in the East* on
Ghengis Khan, glossy periodical publications, museums, historical
theme parks and holidays. As we rush faster and faster towards the
future, so the status and the meaning of history become ever more widely
relevant and contested.

This book also has wider concerns: to explore the nature of history, its
similarities and differences to other human disciplines; how best to
define and understand its mechanics. In doing so, Alex seeks to defend
the position and contribution of Marxism to the task of understanding the
past in terms of the need to change the present.

His material divides into two: what history is not and what it is. The
first chapter of the book looks at the relations between history and philosophy and more specifically whether history can ultimately be reduced
to philosophy. This is an approach to history that claims to find an underlying meaning in the historical process, one that gives it a direction and
unity that stretches across time. The second chapter looks at history as
narrative. Here the book examines an opposite process, one which does
not attempt to discover history's underlying meaning but rather puts
forward the view that historians do nothing more than impose meaning
by ordering events into a causal chain to suit their own ideological purposes. History as narrative is history as stories, all with an equally valid
claim to authenticity, all using the same narratological strategies as
fiction. In rejecting the reductionism of the first and relativism of the
second, the inevitability of the deployment of a wider theoretical account
is posed and this leads to the third chapter.

The constituent elements of a theory of history are examined before
undertaking a comparative evaluation of the two principal contenders,
neo-Weberian historical sociology and historical materialism. One of the
necessary elements of a theory of history, directionality, provides the
centre of the final chapter. The book looks at the underlying patterns of
human history, the degree to which history is an account of human

progress—and the possibility of regression—and the conditions under which it can help in the task of human liberation.

Against the pessimism that pervades much of present intellectual life, Alex sets out to discover 'the rose in the cross of the present'[1] and he follows a variety of paths in search of that rose. Some paths are vital, like the defence of Marxism against the charge of Eurocentrism, some are more enjoyable than others, and some are more peripheral. He seeks to make his argument relevant to current academic debates but in so doing he often tends to argue by proxy, marshalling and juxtaposing a mass of references and materials. This often makes the argument hard to follow. The reader is unsure what side the quoted source is on, and especially so when the target is obscure. On this ground, this book may surely be criticised for academicism. However, it should be remembered that it is published by a commercial publishing house whose target readership has preoccupations not necessarily the same as those of the readership of our journal.

The point that needs to be kept in mind is whether such digressions are obscure or flaw the argument, and, with a little good will, they do not. However, apart from the confusion this technique sometimes produces in the mind of the reader, it sometimes results in the author not leaving himself enough room to speculate or to develop his own ideas. For example, the argument in the first chapter on history as philosophy is conducted in terms of a critique of Fukuyama's thesis of the end of history. One of the latter's two central presuppositions is that the historical process is governed by universal laws and displays patterns analogous to those of individuals' consciousness and their relations between them. A version of this is a projection onto the plane of history of Hegel's master-slave relationship. Alex does make the point that the anthropomorphic view of history—history as the struggle for recognition or as the will to power—concentrates exclusively on the struggle between people/classes and does not take into account the relation/contradiction between the means and relation of production. Therefore this produces a one sided and idealist version of history because all is governed by the 'will to power' or the master-slave relationship and does not integrate it with the material context within which the struggle is carried out. But rather than tackling this reading of the historical process head on—which would have been useful to many readers—Alex pursues his argument by casting doubt on Fukuyama's neo-Hegelian credentials, and then on the contradictions and inconsistencies of those who had influenced him. The result is that, though Fukuyama and Kojève are dissected at length, the argument remains unfocused and the central idea is given much too little space in the last few pages of the chapter.

A recurring theme in the book is the distinction between theory and philosophy of history. The first is the exploration of an open ended causality where the results of conflict are not predetermined. The second traces and retraces a predetermined teleology. Both use empirical evidence, but to diametrically different ends. The former needs it in order to proceed in the process of discovery, relies on it but can never be reduced to it. The latter, on the other hand, uses empirical data but its meaning is reduced to explain a determined 'end' to which history is heading. It thereby effaces 'the distinction between moral judgement and causal explanation'.[2] But how can these two be distinguished from one another? Underlying this opposition is the problem of representation—which requires ordering and therefore selection of information, and of necessity an adoption or exercise of a point of view. Put in another way, the debate is between the inadequacy of relativism versus the limits of objectivity.

The second chapter examines the notion of narrative as a necessary fact of representation, via a discussion of Paul Ricoeur and Hayden White. For Ricoeur, narrative is the organisation of time and events into a causal chain, and is an inevitable human strategy to cope with the experience of living in time and space. But necessary though narrative may be to both history and fiction, Ricoeur does not abandon the distinction between the two. He distinguishes the former on the grounds of its necessarily referential nature. White, on the other hand, is primarily concerned with the pragmatics of narrative, its rhetorical strategies, and he thus effaces the difference between history and fiction.[3]

What makes history different from fiction is neither that history can dispense with the narrative, nor that it can dispense with devices for presenting its material—how things are said to achieve maximum clarity and effect. Rather, argues Alex, the key to distinguishing the one form the other lies in whether what is produced is seen to be ideology or knowledge. In the scientific account, the one that produces knowledge, the narrative is open ended, heuristic ie seeking to uncover experience and explain change. In the ideological account, events are ordered teleologically. This means that history is seen as a sequence of events working towards a set end—like a James Bond movie where all the tests faced by the hero are necessary preludes to his final triumph. Alternativley, events are thought to be hueded by some concealed and unchanging code or set of rules—for example, the struggle between the principles of dictatorship, or a view of history as an eternal competition by some form of natural selection. But if the above is a sufficient criterion to choose between food and bad history, what about the difference between history and fiction?

At this point Alex appears to seek to distinguish fiction from history by drawing a parallel between the former and the conceptual framework of Ancient historiography. He contrasts the characteristic features of history before and after the Enlightenment to show that the first sought to preserve the memory of the past and presupposed the constancy of human nature, the cyclicality of time and the collectivity of experience.[4] In contrast, the second sought to explore the contingent and determinant nature of time and place. And rather than seek in history the re-affirmation of some eternal laws, it critically reconstructed the past guided by the assumption that, 'beyond the differentiation of human history into a multiplicity of social forms each possessing its own idiosyncratic internal logic', human history displays 'an underlying unity'.[5]

The problem here is that Alex does not also provide an account of modern, post-Enlightenment literature. If he did, he would have to show that these qualities are almost precisely the ground on which the novel (which means the new) is usually distinguished from forms of literature developed in precapitalist societies—myth, legend, and tragedy, with the transitional form of the epic.[6] This does not mean that history cannot be distinguished from fiction, but rather that the above does not provide a sufficient basis for such a distinction. And it does not help the argument to introduce the distinguishing criterion of production of knowledge because one of our tradition's most authoritative accounts of the relationship between literature and society, Lukács's critical realism, is based on the criterion of value being precisely the capacity of good fiction to produce knowledge of society.[7] A more sure criterion of differentiation is not the relationship or otherwise with the real, but the forms of its representation. However, even this leads to problems because Alex rightly points out that there is no such thing as one unique and correct historical genre. Therefore it is very difficult to see how one can draw water tight distinctions between the edges of historical studies—such as Ginsburg's *The Cheese and the Worms*—oral history, biography, autobiography and literature.

Alex is very strong in refuting the relativist theory of history, whether it is that of Lyotard or Hayden White, because both base their theories on the non-referentiality of language. He is much weaker when it comes to the distinction between history and fiction because of the difficulty of providing a coherent view of their relationship. The parameters of the issue were recently illustrated by the debate over *Schindler's List*, some attacking it as an impermissible exercise, some for its distortions of reality, while others assumed their position towards the film principally on the grounds of its effect. If we set aside the doubts as to the legitimacy of making such a work of fiction, and the metaphysics of correspondence between discourse and reality, the issue boils down to the question of what makes interpretation of the past possible and why it is desirable.

The answer provided by Alex is that what makes it possible is 'the existence of something in common between the interpreter and the interpreted', whether we are talking about the historian and the past or the reader and historical text.[8] The link is the fact of being human and that which establishes the link between the past and the present, the particular and the general, is theory—and hence theory is inevitable. And the book is very forceful in its establishment of the necessity of a theoretical position, explicit or implicit, which either the historian or the reader of the history must inevitably deploy. But if the common link is the fact of being human, is humanity homogenous? It is precisely because Marxism seeks to build a universal theory of human development that Marxism has been accused—among other things—of Eurocentrism.

The last chapter of the book defends the value of Marxism in providing a perspective that takes into account the particularities of the experience of oppression and struggle either historically or in the present, without at the same time resorting to relativism. The first defence is against the charge of theoretical imperialism. Here Alex is less convincing than elsewhere because he puts forward a defence of realism 'according to which knowledge is arrived at through the construction of a set of theoretical concepts designed to identify the essential structures of the real, which are usually inaccessible to direct observation'. The concept of theory is traceable to the Ancient Greeks but for them it was an essentially contemplative notion. Now, to paraphrase Marx, 'the historians have only interpreted the world in various ways, the point is to change it'. Yet, although Alex stresses that 'knowing nature is inseparable from acting on it', he goes on to try to refute the charge of 'theoretical imperialism' on the grounds that 'the objective of theoretical activity is to establish the essential structure of the real.' The problem with this formulation is that although the 'particular' point of view of an oppressed group can be subsumed within the wider formulation of the 'essential', the bourgeoisie too has a theoretical activity. What makes Marxism desirable is not its greater scientificity compared to bourgeois theory but rather its point of view and its effect, its instrumentality, if you like. Marxism is a theory for a job and in certain domains is proudly and justly inferior to bourgeois 'science'. Either way, however, the argument is concluded with a brilliant critique of political separatism and identity politics and shows that the working class is uniquely able and interested to provide unity and a final outcome to these partial struggles.

Finally, there is the question of irony. The epigraph of the concluding chapter quotes Joseph Conrad: 'Women, children and revolutionaries have no taste for irony'. Irony is the favourite trope of the postmodernist intellectual in which all endeavour is resolved in futility. It is the expression of the pessimism and of the distance of those who think they stand above the 'mêlée' of human conditions. Yet Alex shows that there is a revolutionary irony that also measures distance—the distance between what society could be and what it does, what it says and what people experience, the contradiction between the present potential of humanity and the threat of ever greater misery and destruction. Revolutionaries, like women and children, feel the contradictions of the world but then seek to expose and comprehend them. To do so, their irony measures the forces at work in the world, not from a point of self consciousness but from a point of social consciousness, a political point of view of the agency of social change, the workers. And Alex ends by posing powerfully the notion of class as the organising category for understanding our past and present, and for charting the means of securing our future.

Notes

1   A Callinicos, *Theories and Narratives* (Polity Press, 1995), p14.
2   Ibid, p42.
3   One of the most entertaining parts of the book is where Alex (section 2.2) gives an account of White trying to explain why the Holocaust is not a fiction.
4   Ibid, section 2.2.
5   Ibid, pp64-66.
6   I Watt, *The Rise of the Novel* (Chatto and Windus, 1957), ch 1.
7   G Jenkins, 'Novel Questions', *International Socialism* 62.
8   A Callinicos, op cit, p86.

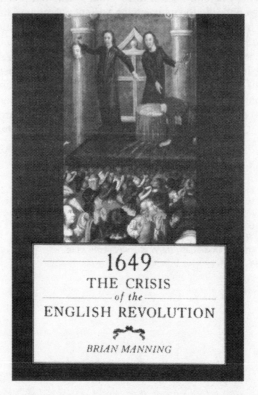

The children of Stalinism

PHIL MARSHALL

Chris Harman's article on Islam, 'The Prophet and the Proletariat', (*International Socialism* 64) has a strength but also several weaknesses. It spells out the contradictory character of what the writer calls 'Islamism', making particularly effective use of recent developments in Algeria to illustrate the point.[1] It makes clear that at base Islamism is a petty bourgeois current whose leaders invariably direct its energies away from the expression of mass interests. But it also leaves some key questions unanswered, notably that of *how* such a vacillating current can draw support in many countries of the Middle East.

How is Islamism able to move outside its usual narrow class limits and, under certain circumstances, build a mass following? Given that the contradictions inherent in the movement are glaring, what allows the Islamists to perform the trick—as, for example, Khomeini did in Iran, as the FIS has done in Algeria, and as Hamas is currently doing in Palestine? This brief response argues that the failure of secular political currents has been a key factor in the making of 'radical' Islam.

For Chris Harman the roots of Islamism are best understood by examining the pattern of economic and social change in the Middle East. The overwhelming emphasis in his article is on uneven development and its impact on urban life, especially the great increase in numbers of urban poor and the impoverishment of some sections of the petty bourgeoisie. It is indeed amongst these frustrated and alienated layers that Islamist currents have had their main influence. But this observation tells us only half the story. As Raymond Hinnebusch has argued of the Islamist movement in Egypt in the 1970s:

> *Its emergence was partly rooted in an accumulation of rapid, unbalanced, social change... But, that the main opposition movement should have taken an Islamic, rather than a secular nationalist or left-wing form, and that it emerged when it did, cannot be explained without a reference to political factors.*[2]

Among such factors are the character of secular nationalism and of Stalinist communism, key components of the ideological context in which Islamism has developed. In fact, it is the record of radical nationalism and of the left across the Middle East which has been the most important political factor in putting modern Islamism on the map.

The mass movements

For 20 years following the Second World War mass movements swept the Middle East. These were not undifferentiated struggles against colonialism but in several cases were insurrectionary movements in which the working class played a key role. In the three main centres of struggle—Egypt, Iran and Iraq—mass mobilisation had its impact in every area of society. Working class organisation positively affected even sections of the petty bourgeoisie, the urban poor and the peasantry which had been under largely conservative influence. A rising level of workers' struggle meant that religious and ethnic communalisms were weakened and that women played a much more prominent role in political life.[3]

The mass movements affected even nationalist regimes which seized power with the aim of weakening such struggles. In Egypt, for example, the Nasser regime was under immense pressure from below—the key reason why it opted for a national development policy which in 1956 produced conflict with the West over Suez. The Suez events in turn generalised support for Nasserism across the region: during the conflict there were mass demonstrations of solidarity, including strikes in the Gulf oilfields. In this radicalised atmosphere the anti-colonial movement in Iraq moved into a situation of revolutionary potential and pro-Western regimes in Lebanon and Jordan came close to collapse. In the late 1950s CIA chief Allen Dulles, seeing the movement sweep towards the Gulf oilfields, described the region as 'the most dangerous place in the world'.[4]

Such developments marginalised Islamism, which had been particularly strong in Egypt, where during the 1930s the Muslim Brotherhood had dominated anti-colonial struggles. Rising levels of working class activity exposed contradictions inherent in the Brotherhood and for the most active workers and students the left became an important pole of attraction. Despite their factionalism and limited Stalinist perspectives, the Communists seemed to hold out a possibility of real political advance which Islamism could not offer.

The experience was repeated across the region. A rising level of struggle had the effect, in particular, of diminishing the importance of communalism—one of the principles on which the European powers had divided the region up into nation states earlier. In Egypt, for example, many of the leaders of the communist organisations of the 1940s and 1950s were Jews; in Iraq activists whose families were of Sunni or Shi'a affiliation or were Kurds or Christians led mass struggles in which their ethnic background was of much less importance than it would have been to earlier generations. Similarly in Iran minority groups supplied many leading members of the workers' movement.

There were negative developments of course. Despite the strength of these movements, in no case was the proletariat able to make a revolutionary breakthrough. In Egypt, Iran and Iraq Communists were projected into leadership of the mass movement but in each case the Stalinist orthodoxy of accommodation to nationalism dictated that revolutionary opportunities should be passed up. In Iraq, for example, the Communist Party (ICP) derailed one of the most powerful mass movements in the Third World. In the late 1950s Iraqi Communists were in an immensely strong position: Hanna Batatu writes that among workers and the poor 'a thrill of hope greeted their rise to great influence'.[5] But the ICP directed its members into the nationalist camp, disorienting the movement and setting the scene for a series of murderous attacks by the Ba'th Party which decimated the ICP and the workers' leadership.

By the mid-1960s the nationalist regime in Iraq was simply one of a series of new Arab state capitalisms which had succeeded in pacifying the workers' movement. Across the region, the left had been reduced to a shadow of the force which seemed to threaten imperialism only years earlier. Stalinism had fetishised the state as a means of bringing change and was now being crushed by the same capitalisms it had helped bring into existence. Joel Beinin's epitaph for the Egyptian Communists could serve for the left across the region. 'Caught up by the embrace of the national movement,' he comments, 'they [were] destroyed by it'.[6]

In 1967, when Israel and its Western allies defeated the Arab armies almost overnight, the nationalist project fell into crisis. The whole notion of building independent states which would be capable of contesting imperialism seemed to have collapsed. Michael Gilsenan comments that in the case of Egypt:

Here was a moment of political and ideological reversal of traumatic propor-
tions... The terms on which 'the nation' had been ideologically constituted
were abruptly revealed as false, illusory, lacking precisely the powers and
capacities they were supposed to enshrine and realise in practice... The
whole logic and symbolism of the nation-state, which had been developed as
the *only authentic language, was undercut and revealed as without substance*
in exactly those dimensions where it had claimed to be most powerful.[7]

Frustrated expectations were soon reflected in a wave of workers' and
students' struggles against the Nasser regime. The prevailing mood was
one in which former left wing activists and a new generation of militant
youth looked for radical solutions—the 'moment of trauma' was also a
moment of opportunity. But the Communist Party had dissolved into the
regime and there was no alternative secular pole of opposition. In these
circumstances even the discredited Islamist movement was able to make
a comeback. Such events set a pattern to be repeated across the region.

Chris Harman's comment that during this period Stalinism was
responsible for 'failure and betrayals' only hints at the massive reverse
suffered by the workers' movement at the hands of the left.[8] In fact, by
the late 1960s communist strategy had evacuated the Middle East of any
coherent secular alternative to nationalism—and had done so at a time
when the region was about to move into a period of increased instability.
This left an increasingly disillusioned population without a point of reference for change and opened a political space which religious activism
soon started to occupy.

Palestine

The left had already set out a practice that positively encouraged the
growth of alternative political currents: it had prepared the ground for
Islamism. A key issue was that of Palestine. One striking omission from
Chris Harman's article is any reference to the importance of Palestine
within Middle East politics. In fact, it has been a key mobilising issue for
Islamism and one which has shown the left in an even worse light than
the nationalists.

Even before the establishment of Israel, the left had failed to identify
the Zionist movement as one inextricably linked to Western interests. In
1947, when Moscow declared in favour of a Jewish state, the bulk of the
left in the region was hopelessly confused and when war broke out in
1948 it was the Muslim Brotherhood which provided concrete support
for Palestinian guerrilla resistance. Even those communists who identified with the Palestinians eventually accepted Moscow's pro-Zionist
stance: as Beinin notes, for Arab communists, 'Soviet support for the
creation of Israel superseded their historic objections to Zionism'.[9]

It was only in the mid-1950s, when Moscow reoriented towards the Arab states, that Communist Parties began to talk of a connection between Israel and Western imperialism. Even this abrupt change was double edged: it was part of the swing into uncritical support for nationalist regimes that allowed Arab Communist leaders to declare, bizarrely, that nationalist dictators such as Nasser represented 'the [Communist] party in power'.[10]

In the early 1960s Nasser announced that he had 'no plan' for Palestine; the left did not dissent, nor did it oppose establishment of the Palestine Liberation Organisation (PLO), set up in 1964 with the aim of containing the increasingly subversive Palestinian national movement. The question of Israel now became one of the key issues on which a weak and still marginal Islamist movement began to make headway. The leading Egyptian Islamist Sayyid Qutb, for example, attacked the regime and the left for betrayal of the Palestinian cause, portraying the Communists as 'the secret ally of Zionism'.[11] There were particularly bitter criticisms of the Arab Communist Parties for maintaining closer links with the Israeli left, itself organically linked to the Zionist state, than they did with the Palestinian masses.[12]

In the wake of Arab defeat in 1967, the Islamists discovered that they had a huge new audience. They maintained that secular nationalists and the left were weak and corrupt; only by reasserting Islamic values could Arab society liberate Palestine. Walid Abdelnasser observes how these arguments 'religionised' the whole question of conflict with Israel and the West:

> *Arabs were defeated because they lacked piety, while 'Jews' won the war because they fought it on a religious basis... The Islamic movement was satisfied that the 1967 defeat brought to Arabs an element of religionisation of the conflict with Israel, and that it led to the decline of national and secular influences in the region and to the revival of the Islamic alternative.*[13]

Communalism

In failing to tackle the question of Palestine, the left had sold the pass on the key expression of the national question in the region. It went on to capitulate on every other related issue, notably on that of communalism.

Despite the disastrous outcome of earlier popular front strategies, during the 1960s Moscow directed Communist parties in Syria and (for a second time) in Iraq to join nationalist regimes, and attempted similar manoeuvres in Sudan and Lebanon. The left in these countries now argued for embrace of the same sectarianisms which had once been contested as a matter of principle. In Syria and Iraq, for example, communists entered Ba'thist regimes based respectively on the minority Alawi and Arab Sunni communities. The left endorsed sectarianisms rooted in differences of language, 'ethnicity' and religion—the very divisions implemented by colonialism and which had been successfully weakened by the mass movements of the 1940s and 1950s.

This had grotesque results. In Syria the CPS declared the Ba'th Party to be one of the 'basic revolutionary forces' in the Arab world, one which it said had adopted 'scientific socialism'.[14] It then entered an increasingly sectarian regime, surrendering all political independence. In Iraq the ICP also aligned with the Ba'th, now presented by Communist leaders as a 'revolutionary' force, and soon found itself party to a savage war against the Kurds and repression of the Shiites. The Communists thereby strengthened communal divisions and suspicions, creating a political climate in which ideologies such as Islamism could prosper. By the 1970s both Syria and Iraq had seen rapid growth of Islamist movements which had hitherto been insignificant in national politics.

As partners in the nationalist regimes, communists were also complicit in systematic attacks on the Palestinian movement. They were implicated in the Arab betrayal of the PLO during Black September 1970 and the onslaught in Lebanon in 1975. They were also party to the cynical use of guerrilla organisations within the Palestinian national movement to serve the regimes' own ends. This helped to isolate Palestinians from wider struggles within the region and to guarantee the series of defeats which ended with expulsion from Lebanon in 1982, marking the demise of the PLO as a mass armed resistance movement.

Communism and Islamism

By the early 1970s hitherto marginalised Islamist currents had started to make headway in Egypt, Syria, Iraq, Iran and Algeria. To the extent that the language of nationalism was seen to have failed, the language of Islam became a means of expressing opposition to the state, to Israel and to the West. The Islamist organisations were dominated by petty bourgeois concerns and were vacillating, inconsistent and often divisive. Many were compromised by their own relationships to the regimes; all were in some sense communalist in that they called for unity of Muslims vis-a-vis other religious groups or even other Islamic sects. Most of the Islamic oppositions, however, had become the sole focus for national political activity and their growth provoked a further crisis for the left, which showed itself incapable of comprehending the religious revival.

The international Communist movement had long since abandoned the approach to political Islam which had been adopted by revolutionary Marxists during and after the Russian Revolution of 1917. Then Lenin had been the key figure in identifying the need to understand the contradictory character of nationalist movements in the 'colonial' world, including those under religious influence such as the Islamic movements of Central Asia. In 1920 the Comintern's *Theses on the National and Colonial Questions*, drafted by Lenin, set out a series of principles for communist relations with national movements. They argued specifically against compromise with the Islamists and for 'the need to combat pan-Islamism and similar trends, which strive to combine the liberation movement against European and American imperialism with an attempt to strengthen the position of the khans, landowners and mullahs, etc'.[15]

Nonetheless, Lenin maintained, it was necessary to support Islamist movements under conditions in which they contested local ruling classes and/or colonial control. On this basis, the Bolsheviks argued for collaboration with the pan-Islamist Jadid movement. This 'astonishing alliance' was defended by Lenin with great vigour against those who believed that communists should have no dealings with a religious activism.[16] He argued that it was vital to persuade such movements in the 'colonial' world that their future lay with the workers of Europe against the imperial powers and that a dual approach was required—both 'against' and 'for' such movements in measures determined by the specific circumstances.[17]

Within a few years, however, the Stalinised Comintern had abandoned these internationalist principles. This was itself a contributory factor in weakening the secular wing of the anti-colonial movement across the Middle East and in producing the Islamist revival which began in the late 1920s with the establishment of the Muslim Brotherhood. In fact it was the Brotherhood which the Stalinised Communist Parties of the Arab world subsequently both attacked and courted on an entirely opportunistic basis.

From the late 1920s the Communist parties' line zig-zagged according to Moscow's latest preoccupation. This was particularly evident in the case of Islamism. In the 1940s, for example, with communists making every effort to establish popular fronts with the nationalists, Islam was often presented as 'revolutionary'. The Lebanese communist Raif Khoury wrote:

> *Do you remember, each time you hear the echo of that pristine call, that* **Alluhu akbar** *means, in plain language: punish the greedy usurers! Tax those who accumulate profits! Confiscate the profits of the thieving monopolists! Guarantee bread to the people! Open the road of education and progress to women! Destroy all the vermin who spread ignorance and division among the community!*[18]

Khoury went on to argue that the emergence of Islam in the 7th century was part of the same continuous historical process that had produced the October revolution. Muslim political activists could therefore be viewed as 'progressives' little different from communists themselves. This position could easily be changed, however, when Islamists clashed with the left. The popular front approach then allowed that they could be declared 'fascist'.[19] Such opportunistic attitudes were carried into the post-colonial era, so that by the 1950s Egyptian communists, for example, were able to move casually in and out of alliances with the Muslim Brotherhood.[20] When, a decade later, religious activism began to revive, the left was incapable of making an assessment of its real political character—one reason why some former communists and communist sympathisers moved so easily into the Islamist camp.

Islamist revival

Islamism has been shaped within a political environment dominated by the failures of secular nationalism and Stalinism. Its advance is intimately linked with the retreat of these movements; it is not, therefore, merely a product of uneven development but the result of an interaction of economic, social and political factors within which the question of ideas has been of enormous importance.

Thus Alex Callinicos has been right to argue that:

> *The left throughout the Middle East is bankrupt—above all because of the influence of Stalinism which encouraged, for example, the Palestinian resistance to put its faith in 'progressive' Arab regimes rather than in the workers and peasants of the region. Consequently, in country after country Islamic fundamentalism has filled the vacuum, appealing especially to the urban poor as an apparently radical anti-imperialist ideology.*[21]

This pattern becomes even clearer when we examine situations in which Islamists have made the most rapid advance. In Egypt the events of the late 1960s put Islamism back on the agenda. Hinnebusch comments:

> *It is clear that the decisive political event which revived the fortunes of the Islamic movement was the 1967 defeat...the people's faith in Nasir as a symbol of Arab dignity and strength and in the secular nationalist and socialist mix which made up his ideology, was shattered, leaving a leadership and ideological vacuum.*[22]

It was not inevitable, however, that the vacuum should be filled by the ideas of religious activism. In fact, the decade after the war saw a series of mass struggles during which conditions could hardly have been more congenial for the left. Initially the Islamist current grew only slowly—it was as if the secular alternative was being tested to the limit before there could be a turn to religious activism. But the left failed to meet this challenge, remaining what Fawzi Mansour calls 'an apologetic appendage' of the state,[23] and in the absence of any political alternative Egypt's Islamists began to build a mass base.[24]

A similar pattern is evident in Iran. In the early 1950s the Tudeh (Communist) Party reacted to defeat of the mass movement by declaring Iranian workers unready for change and going into hibernation—it announced a policy of 'inactive survival'.[25] This dismissive attitude to the working class was absorbed by the guerrillaist currents which emerged in the 1960s among young people convinced that they, rather than the working class, could be the agency of change. When the movement against the Shah emerged in 1977, culminating in the mass strikes of 1978-1979, the left was merely an observer.

The record of the left in such countries is often put down to problems presented by repression. In a number of recent analyses of the Iranian revolution, liberal and left wing Iranian academics have sought to show that secular forces were simply overwhelmed by the Pahlavi state. Mansoor Moaddel, for example, argues that during the 1960s and 1970s, 'the radical groups had been debilitated by state repression, many of their leaders had been either killed during armed clashes with the security forces or imprisoned, and the remaining cadres and members were too few to be able to mobilise the masses along the social revolutionary line'.[26]

This avoids facing the brute facts imposed by Stalinism: that as in the Arab world, the left in Iran had no 'social revolutionary line', having abandoned the notion of independent working class activity. Despite the fact of repression, the Iranian guerrillas had an enormous potential audience, one they self consciously dismissed. It was only after 25 years of retreat by secular radicals that Khomeini and his supporters, hitherto largely confined to the 'ulema and the bazaar, were able to make their breakthrough into the urban poor, the professionals and even into sections of the working class, giving the Islamists their chance to co-opt the revolutionary movement.[27]

Such cases show how Islamism grows amid the decay of nationalism and Stalinism, reproducing the latter's authoritarianism and elitism (and often intensifying them) but surviving because the crisis of political leadership has reached such critical levels.

What is Islamism?

Chris Harman does not characterise Islamism as a specific social and political force, although he hints that it is not a nationalism. I believe that this is a mistake: the development of Islamism suggests that it *is* one of currents which has emerged within Third World nationalism, albeit at the conservative end of the nationalist spectrum. Unless we see it in this way, the emergence of the Muslim Brotherhood in the 1930s within the anti-colonial movement is incomprehensible; so too in the 'post-colonial' era, with 'Khomeinism' emerging as part of the challenge to the Shah, and Islamism appearing as the most vigorous element within the Palestinian movement. Indeed, it has been a costly failure of Stalinism that Communist leaderships have been unable to identify religious activism in such terms.

Radical nationalism, Stalinism and Islamism are closely related—one reason why the latter has often been able to grow at the expense of the former without disturbing the structures of the political system. Initially such growth may be slow but if mass opposition develops against the background of a weak or discredited left some sections of society will be attracted to ideas which repeat the themes of secular radicalism— mobilisation against 'external' enemies, 'guided' change, and the orientation on the state—but do so in Islamic idiom. Olivier Roy maintains that this is no less than an imitation of the left, in which ideas are borrowed from the Communist strategy and then 'injected with Quranic terminology'.[28]

In this sense Islamic activism has operated at the political level as a nationalism apparently invigorated by religious belief. It has not been a break with the pattern of secular politics but an extension of it—one which promises to implement much the same strategies that radical nationalism and Stalinism have deserted.[29]

As Nazih Ayubi has observed of Egyptian Islamism in the 1960s and 1970s, the movement did not mark a break from Nasserism but was 'a mirror image of the Nasserist project, revolving similarly around the state and regarding the act of government as the main approach to changing society'.[30] So too in Iran, where Islamist ideologues such as Ali Shari'ati attempted a fusion of social democratic and Islamist ideas which has sometimes been called an Islamic 'Marxism'.[31] In the case of Algeria, Hugh Roberts has argued that in the 1980s the FIS emerged as 'the offspring of the [nationalist] FLN, a real chip off the old block'.[32]

Islamism is a 'cousin' of the petty bourgeois nationalisms which have preceded its recent revival. The relationship is close although the two currents are not identical. Even during the colonial period Islamism was a conservative nationalism, reflecting the concerns of a leadership drawn from petty bourgeois layers connected to commercial capital and landowning interests, and which has been implacably hostile to indepen-dent action from below. Radical nationalism has usually had somewhat different roots, its leaders emerging from the state bureaucracy and the new middle class and sometimes responding to pressures exerted by the mass movement.

There is confirmation of this pattern in Palestine, where until recently the Islamist presence within the national movement was negligible. Only since the failure of the *intifada* under the suffocating influence of Yasser Arafat have Hamas and Islamic Jihad really made headway. Disintegration of secular nationalism and the ineffectiveness of the Palestinian left have allowed religious activists to capture a large audience—indeed, leaders of Hamas have expressed their surprise at how easily they have been able to make progress merely by putting an Islamic gloss on Arafat's strategy.[33]

The sort of activists drawn to radical Islamism across the Middle East are those who, in an earlier generation, made up the cadre of the left. Few Islamist recruits show the systematic religiosity said to constitute 'piety'; indeed, this constitutes one of the chief complaints of leaders of the Islamist movements.[34] Many Muslim activists gravitate towards a cause which alone seems to offer them a challenge to the state. It is in this sense that they should be seen as the Islamist children of Stalinism.

Conclusion

In 1922 Lenin argued that the issue of relations with the Islamic move-ment in Asia constituted 'a worldwide question' for the international workers' movement.[35] The judgement proved to be prophetic. When Stalinism defeated the Russian working class and abandoned the Comintern approach it virtually guaranteed emergence of a new religious activism in those regions in which Islam could operate as an idiom for the expression of national aspirations. In the 'post-colonial' era, Islamism has continued to fill the spaces vacated by the left.[36] Today's Marxists need not only to combat the state, and the ideological influence of Islamism, but the legacy of Stalinism, which has played a decisive role in putting religion back on the map.

There is now a real opportunity for revolutionary Marxists to point the way forward. Everywhere Islamism has failed to deliver. The Egyptian *gama'at islamiyya*, a mass organisation in the 1970s, has been all but wiped out as an active force in the country's major cities. The Algerian FIS is involved in a civil war in which its armed groups do no more than imitate the substitutionism which cost Iran's guerrillas mass support. In Palestine, Hamas seeks deals in the hope of sharing power in Fatah's 'Arafatistan'. Meanwhile, Iran's Islamic Republic and Sudan's

Muslim Brotherhood regimes are parodies of the self-serving, violent regimes which preceded them.

Revolutionary Marxism can provide a perspective which offers mass action on the basis of wholly independent workers' parties, of internationalism and intransigent opposition to communalism. The hidden history of mass struggles in the Middle East provides the confidence required to pursue this perspective. It shows above all that the political potential of the working class is not in question. What is at issue is the negative and ultimately destructive tradition of Stalinist political leadership.

Notes

1   In this article I have used both 'Islamism' and 'Islamic activism' to refer to modern movements which use Islamic vocabulary and traditions to set out strategies aimed at social and political change.
2   R Hinnebusch, *Egyptian Politics Under Sadat* (Cambridge, 1985), p199.
3   On Iran see E Abrahamian, *Iran Between Two Revolutions* (Princeton, 1982), pp347-371; on Egypt see J Beinin and Z Lockman, *Workers on the Nile* (Princeton, 1987), ch X; on Iraq see H Batatu, *The Old Social Classes and the Revolutionary Movements of Iraq* (Princeton, 1978), bk 3.
4   Quoted in F Hazelton, 'Iraq to 1963', in CARDRI, *Saddam's Iraq* (London, 1986), p26.
5   H Batatu, op cit, pp898-899.
6   J Beinin, 'The Communist Movement and National Political Discourse in Nasirist Egypt', in *The Middle East Journal*, vol 41, no 4, 1987, p577.
7   M Gilsenan, 'Popular Islam and the State in Contemporary Egypt,' in F Halliday and H Alavi, *State and Ideology in the Middle East and Pakistan* (London, 1988), pp173-174.
8   C Harman, 'The Prophet and the Proletariat', *International Socialism* 64, p25.
9   J Beinin, *Was the Red Flag Flying There?* (London, 1990), p145.
10 As in a declaration from the Egyptian Communist Party to its members in Nasser's prison camps, quoted in Beinin (1987), p577.
11 W Abdelnasser, *The Islamic Movement in Egypt* (London, 1994), p173.
12 Ibid, p177.
13 Ibid, p120.
14 M S Agwani, *Communism in the Arab East* (Bombay, 1969), p52.
15 B Hessel (ed), *Theses, Resolutions and Manifestos of the First Four Congresses of the Third International* (London, 1980), p80.
16 H Carrere d'Encausse, *Islam and the Russian Empire* (London, 1988), p187.
17 Ibid, p188.
18 Quoted in M Rodinson, *Marxism and the Muslim World* (London, 1979), p31.
19 A good example from Egypt is provided in A Abdalla, *The Student Movement and National Politics in Egypt* (London, 1985), p59.
20 In 1954, with the Soviet Union still suspicious of the Nasser regime, Moscow told Egyptian communists that the Muslim Brotherhood should be treated as 'the most anti-imperialist force in the country'. W Abdelnasser, op cit, p54.
21 A Callinicos, *Marxism and the National Question* (London, 1989), p18.
22 R Hinnebusch, op cit, p199.
23 F Mansour, *The Arab World: Nation, State and Democracy* (London, 1992), p103.

24 By the late 1970s the *gama'at islamiyya* (Islamic groups) had a membership estimated at 100,000. R Hinnebusch, op cit, p205.

25 E Abrahamian, op cit, p456.

26 M Moaddel, *Class, Politics and Ideology in the Iranian Revolution* (New York, 1993), p161.

27 Moaddel's history of the revolution, which Chris Harman cites extensively, is a typical 'revisionist' account. The author rejects class conflict as the motor force in historical change in favour of 'discourse', commenting that in the Iranian Revolution, 'The overthrow of the monarchy did not originate from the dynamic of the interests, opportunity and solidarity structures of the diverse classes and groups involved in the Iranian Revolution. There was nothing [sic] inherent in the interests and organisation of the bazaar and workers that necessitated the overthrow of the regime in a revolutionary manner... The revolutionary crisis began when the social discontent was expressed in terms of Shi'i revolutionary discourse.' (M Moaddel, op cit. p 268). This conceals both the scale of mass activity in the revolutionary movement and the suicidal conduct of the left.

Similar apologies for communist strategy are apparent in even the best accounts of the working class movement and the left: for example, in Abrahamian's excellent *Iran Between Two Revolutions*, in which the author concludes that a significant factor in Khomeini's success among Iranian workers 'was the vacuum created by the [Pahlavi] regime when it systematically destroyed all the secular opposition parties' (E Abrahamian 1982, op cit, p536). In fact, the parties had not been destroyed but all had effectively removed themselves from active engagement in working class life.

28 O Roy, *The Failure of Political Islam* (London, 1994), p3.

29 Aziz al-Azmeh makes an important observation about the relationship between Islamism and secular nationalism in the Arab world when he comments that modern Islamism can be seen as 'a kind of hypernationalism which is unthinkable without the legacy of Arab nationalist ideology'. A al-Azmeh, *Islams and Modernities* (London, 1993), p82.

30 N Ayubi, *Political Islam* (London, 1991), p142.

31 See the assessment of Shari'ati in S Zubaida, *Islam, the People and the State* (London, 1989), p25.

32 H Roberts, 'Doctrinaire Economics and Political Opportunism in the Strategy of Algerian Islamism', in J Ruedy, *Islam and Secularism in North Africa* (London, 1994), p140.

33 Ziad Abu-Amr notes, 'The Society [of the Muslim Brothers—ie Hamas] has realised that it did not require much to establish itself as a serious contender and rival to the PLO and as a source of trouble to the Israeli occupation.' Z Abu-Amr, *Islamic Fundamentalism in the West Bank and Gaza* (London, 1994), p89.

34 Umar 'abd al-Rahman, a leading figure of the Egyptian *gama'at*, is particularly scathing about the quality of the group's recruits, whom he alleges have been almost totally unfamiliar with the religious texts and principles which are supposed to guide their political activity. N Ayubi, op cit, p80.

35 Quoted in H Carrere d'Encausse, op cit, p188.

36 Chris Harman's comment on the approach of Marxists to national movements in the colonial and post-colonial periods (C Harman, op cit, n52, p60) blurs the issue of how to approach Islamism today. He argues that in a world of capitalist states integrated into an international system petty bourgeois movements such as Islamism are compromised by their relations with local capital and cannot be approached in the same way as earlier anti-colonial movements.

The position of revolutionary Marxists on this question should always be based on an evaluation of the concrete circumstances. Here the case of Palestine is instructive, for in Israel the West sustains an aggressive settler state which mirrors colonial structures and has generalised the national question throughout the region. Palestinian responses have been influenced by both secular and Islamist currents, each of which has been compromised by its relationship to local capital (arguably more completely in the case of the largely secular PLO). This should not prevent revolutionary Marxists maintaining a position of critical support for Palestinian struggles to the extent that they express the aspiration for self determination. The emphasis is on the *critical* character of such support: it is this that the Stalinist tradition has abandoned at such cost and which has been so important in feeding the illusion that a conservative current such as Islamism can effectively confront Zionism and the West.

Bookwatch: 100 years of cinema

PAUL D'AMATO

In March 1895 two French entrepreneurs, the Lumière brothers, gave private screenings of their first film, *Workers Leaving the Lumière Factory*. In the same year in the United States the Latham brothers projected a film about boxing to a paying audience. The great commercial potential of films—first shown to patrons individually as 90 second scenes inside viewing machines at 'penny arcades'—was apparent from the beginning. Worldwide, the film industries of the US, France, Britain and Germany quickly became big businesses, as millions of people flocked to see the new form of entertainment.

The Russian revolutionary Leon Trotsky, speaking in 1923, summarised the immense power and potential of the cinema:

This amazing spectacular innovation has cut into human life with a successful rapidity never experienced in the past. In the daily life of capitalist towns, the cinema has become just such an integral part of life as the bath, the beer-hall, the church... The passion for the cinema is rooted in the desire for distraction, the desire to see something new and improbable, to laugh and to cry, not at your own, but at other people's misfortunes. The cinema satisfies these demands in a very direct, visual, picturesque, and vital way... That is why the audience bears such a grateful love to the cinema, that inexhaustible font of impressions and emotions.

In the struggle to build a socialist Russia, Trotsky called cinema a 'weapon, which cries out to be used'.[1]

The impact of the cinema described by Trotsky, while more often than not proscribed by the limitations of filmmaking as a mass industry under capitalism, is best exemplified by Serge Eisenstein's classic *Battleship Potemkin*, a path breaking film about a mutiny on a battleship during the 1905 revolution. A good short biography of his life and work, *Eisenstein: the Growth of a Cinematic Genius,* tells how in 1933 the crew of a Dutch battleship in Indonesia claimed at their court martial for mutinying that their actions were inspired by Eisenstein's film.[2]

In their history of 100 years, from silents to the 'talkies', from TV to the advent of cable and the video cassette recorder, films, and in particular Hollywood films, continue to remain among the most popular form of entertainment worldwide. Hundreds of books have been written on the cinema, most of them on Hollywood. They range from the pulp biography (there are at least three I noticed on the shelves about Elizabeth Taylor alone), and the movie goer guide—the latter two types being the most popular—to serious histories and academic books on film theory and criticism. With prior apologies, this bookwatch will focus on, but not be limited to, books about American film, only because that is what I know best.

Most of what we read about films comes from popular reviews that talk mainly about plots and acting. To learn about how films are put together (their form), their technological development, about film as a mass industry and mass entertainment, you have to delve a little deeper than *Halliwell's Film Guide* and *Halliwell's Filmgoers' Companion*. Nevertheless, these two books are among the most useful for cross-referencing information when you're watching a film on television. Say you're watching a Hollywood film—you think it's probably from the 1970s—starring Faye Dunaway and Jack Nicholson, about a private detective in Los Angeles who gets too deeply into a murder investigation and uncovers filthy corruption and greed in the highest places. You don't know the film's name, so you use the *Companion* and cross-reference the films that Dunaway and Nicholson both starred in. Bingo, you discover the film is probably *Chinatown*. You look up *Chinatown* in the *Film Guide*, and you discover it was directed by Roman Polanski in 1974. The guide, however, is marred by the author's snobbish disdain towards anything that wasn't produced during Hollywood's 'golden age', dismissing *Chinatown*, for example, as a 'pretentious melodrama'.[3]

For a more general overview of film—its origins, technical and historical development, and place in society—there are a few good books to start with. Gerald Mast's standard text, *A Short History of the Movies*,[4] is the most thorough, recently updated to encompass the origins of film, through the Hollywood heydays of the 1920s, 1930s and 1940s; the industry's decline and crisis in the 1950s and 1960s with the advent of television and the breakup of the studio system; to Hollywood's revival in the mid-1970s, the barren high tech 'blockbuster' driven 1980s, right up to the more eclectic 1990s. It is at its best detailing how films began and developed in Europe and the United States and has excellent chapters on the development of European cinema, including chapters on the great early Soviet filmmakers like Eisenstein and Pudovkin, as well as chapters on the innovative post-Second World War 'new wave' of Italian and French cinema which brought us directors like Truffaut, Goddard, Antonioni and Fellini.

Books on Hollywood

Since 1920 Hollywood has held a central place in the world film industry, not least because it perfected a means to produce cheap, popular formula entertainment easily accessible to millions. By 1915 US film producers controlled 80 percent of the world's film market, and Hollywood reached its peak of popularity and profitability shortly after the Second World War. Most of the post-war period leading up to the early 1970s were, economically if not artistically, crisis years for Hollywood, but the advent of video and cable television has produced a massive revival of fortunes for the film industry since the mid-1970s.

There is no doubt that, as a mass industry producing commodities for mass entertainment, Hollywood executives have striven to produce a product that will appeal to the largest audience and offend the fewest, based upon tried and tested formulas which leave little room for experiment and unfettered creativity: films, therefore, which reflect to a large extent the ruling ideas of society. But films depend upon a mass audience, subject to historical shifts in moods and consciousness. That contradiction has meant that Hollywood has produced and continues to produce interesting films with limited insights. Robert Sklar's *Movie Made America: A Cultural History of American Movies*, probably the best single volume history of Hollywood, makes that clear by weaving together an economic, social and political analysis of the development of film technology, filmmaking techniques, subject matter and audience.[5] He emphasises that from the beginning in the US films developed as a form of mass entertainment for the working class. Of the first mass produced and distributed films in the first decade and a half of this century, the majority, Sklar points out, were slapstick comedies that spoofed authority figures and institutions—'cops, schools, marriage, middle-class manners, all the fundamental institutions of the social order, were made to look as foolish and inane as the lowlife characters'.[6] We learn also in Sklar's book that in the early 1990s Hollywood became the main site for movie production not simply because of the warm, even climate and variety of terrain in Southern California, but because Los Angeles was at the time an open shop town—movie producers moved there to escape unions.

Both Mast's and Sklar's books depart from many other general histories about film in that they take the time to look at how filmmaking techniques developed. From both, you get a fascinating look at how the movie camera was first used as the equivalent of a spectator in a vaudeville hall. The first films simply recorded, in one shot and within a fixed area, a natural event or staged action. Later, shots were spliced together to show a sequence of actions, and still later, Edwin Porter and the notorious D W Griffith would develop and refine techniques taken for granted today—varying the length and distance of shots to the action, varying the angle of shots, cross-cutting between more than one action, and so on. Eisenstein was heavily influenced by Griffith in his development of the theory of 'montage'—the idea that film meaning was conveyed by the juxtaposition of different shots.

There are several other excellent books that cover more specific areas of Hollywood's history. Thomas Shatz's *The Genius of the System: Hollywood Filmmaking in the Studio Era* is the best overview of the period of Hollywood at its height of power and prestige, when a handful of companies controlled a fully integrated system of production and distribution.[7] Victor Navasky's *Naming Names,* although weighed down with excessive detail and marred by an anguished preoccupation with the personal reasons for why some actors, writers and directors in Hollywood 'named names' during the McCarthy era in the late 1940s, is a useful history of that period. He shows the devastating effect the anti-Communist witch hunts had not only on the hundreds of individuals whose careers were destroyed, but on the character and content of films (though the book spends little time on the films themselves).[8] More interesting in its account of how the climate of class struggle produced stirrings among Hollywood's writers who organised the Screen Writers Guild is Nancy Lynn Schwartz's *Hollywood Writers' Wars,* which provides a useful backdrop for the onslaught of the anti-Communist crusade that came soon after.[9] A useful but sketchy overview of the political directors and films of Hollywood between 1930 and the 1960s can be found in *Film and Politics in America: A Social Tradition.*[10]

There are a couple of good books on the post-war decline and revival of Hollywood. Michael Pye and Lynda Myles's *The Movie Brats* focuses on the directors who were at the centre of Hollywood's resurgence in the 1970s, both commercially and creatively—Coppola, Scorcese, DePalma, Lucas and Spielberg.[11] Many of them got their start working at Roger

Corman's American International Pictures, infamous producer of the cheap horror/slasher/science fiction/bikers from hell films of the 1960s which catered to bored suburban youth. *Brats* is best at showing how these directors showed both the potential and tremendous limitations of Hollywood filmmaking. In the early 1970s, in the wake of the 1960s upheaval and severe crisis in Hollywood (summarised by studio bigwig William Goldman's saying, 'Nobody knows anything'), there was a creative space to make films like *The Godfather* (which became the first massive hit for Hollywood in years), *Mean Streets* and *The Conversation*. That space quickly closed up in the mid-1970s as Spielberg's *Jaws* and Lucas's *Star Wars* films proved that enormous amounts of money could be made from fast paced, high tech fantasy 'blockbusters'.

Stephen Bach's *Final Cut: Dreams and Disaster in the Making of Heaven's Gate*, takes us through the making of the film by Michael Cimino (of *Deer Hunter* fame) which at the time was the greatest financial disaster in Hollywood's history (costing $44 million—peanuts by today's *Waterworld* standards), bringing down United Artists and prompting a complete reorganisation of the industry's top personnel in the early 1980s.[12]

Final Cut gives you a good sense of how the conflict between the increased creative leeway given to some directors in the late 1970s and the studio's needs for assured profit flow came to a head around *Heaven's Gate*. Cimino, in choosing as his subject the battle of immigrant farmers struggling against avaricious cattle barons in Wyoming, didn't exactly ingratiate himself to the producers, who, alarmed at the mounting costs and length of the film, sabotaged its release. The film has been alternately praised as a masterpiece and denounced as a sprawling mess—and it is perhaps a little of both.

Shatz has also written an essay which covers the development of Hollywood from the 1940s to the 1990s which can be found in *Film Theory Goes to the Movies*, a book which also has some interesting analysis of contemporary films like Spike Lee's *Jungle Fever* and John Singleton's *Boyz'n the Hood*, although the book is full of annoying film theory jargon.[13]

Other books

Film as a Subversive Art by Amos Vogel, written in the early 1970s, is a good introduction to the history of more left wing and less mainstream films. With short essays interspersed with short synopses of films from around the world considered either in form or content to be on the cutting edge of the art, Vogel moves from the films produced in Russia after the revolution through the development of the Maoist Avant Garde in the late 1960s and beyond. Vogel praises the 'towering achievements' of the Russian filmmakers shortly after the 1917 revolution, citing the 'liberating, innovative tendencies freed by the liquidation of the former regime, the exuberant hopes for the creation of a first society of equality and freedom'.[14]

An excellent short book, *Cinema in Revolution*, tells the story of that period of intense creativity in Russia through essays and reminiscences of the great Russian filmmakers themselves: Serge Eisenstein, Dziga Vertov, Alexander Dovzhenko and others.[15] Barna's book on Eisenstein, mentioned earlier, shows how that initial period of creativity gave way to the rise of Stalinism that crushed the creative impulse almost as quickly as it rose. Stalin apparently took a keen interest in film, even visiting studios to watch the editing process. In a late night visit to Eisenstein's studio, Stalin ordered several hundred metres of film removed from Eisenstein's 1929 film *October,* saying to the director, 'Lenin's liberalism no longer applies'.[16]

Film theory and criticism

Most film theory is written by people who have nothing to do with films—more often than not academics. The exception is some of the early Russian directors, and particularly Eisenstein. His book, *Film Form: Essays in Film Theory,* develops his theory of 'montage'.[17] Vogel's synopsis of Eisenstein's first film, *Strike,* describes beautifully how Eisenstein's concept of montage ('the art of conflict between images') worked in practice:

> *The best example of Eisenstein's montage methods occurs in the famous sequence in which the four capitalists dealing with the strike are seated in the plush comfort and isolation of their mansion, smoking and drinking. Through cross-cutting, we now see, in this order: workers at a clandestine strike meeting; the capitalist putting a lemon into a juice extractor; the workers discuss their demands; the handle of the juice extractor descends to crush the fruit; the workers are charged by mounted police; the boss says in an intertitle: 'Crush hard and then squeeze!'; the workers are attacked; a piece of lemon drops on the well polished shoe of the capitalist; disgusted, he uses the paper containing the workers' demands to wipe it off.*[18]

If most film criticism takes the form of reviews of plot and acting, film theory has gone the other way, emphasising not content but form— the language of film. This is an important starting point, since what makes films unique as a form of art or entertainment is the particular way in which they are put together. Nevertheless, much film theory has forgotten to reintegrate an analysis of the structure of films with content—what it is they convey. This meant for example that radicalised critics and filmmakers in the 1960s, rejecting the pat formulas of the Hollywood style narrative film, believed that simply making films which subverted the dominant conceptions of how to make a film constituted a subversion of the social order.

Modern film theory emerged from the upheavals of the late 1960s. It has been heavily influenced by Louis Althusser, and later by 'semiotics', 'Structuralism' and 'post-structuralism'. While it began, in however distorted a way (influenced as it was by Maoist idealism) to challenge the dominant methods and themes of cinema, it has become thoroughly absorbed into academia as film departments have sprang up in various universities and the political climate in Europe and the US has shifted to the right. Moreover, one of the results of the influence of Althusser and the Structuralists on film theory has been to see not only films, but film theory itself, as a form of 'theoretical practice', and therefore a 'site' of struggle to change society. Not only does this overestimate the impact of films on society as a whole, it helped justify the retreat from the class struggle into the ivory tower of academia; you could be a complacent academic talking to other complacent academics in an obscure jargon and still believe yourself to be engaging in a struggle to change society.

The best place to start with film theory is the standard text by Mast and Cohen, *Film Theory and Criticism*, which excerpts writings and essays by early film theorists like Eisenstein, Krakauer and Bazin, as well as writings on the now famous 'auteur' theory (that directors are authors of movies like writers are authors of books). It also includes an interesting and influential essay by Walter Benjamin, *The Work of Art in the Age of Mechanical Reproduction*.[19]

Unfortunately now out of print, Colin Sparks's essay 'A Marxist Guide to Contemporary Film Theory' in *International Socialism* 34, is an excellent introduction to film theory from a Marxist standpoint.[20] As he points out, one of the results of the influence of Structuralism in film theory has been to deny that there is a single, Marxist (or any other) method of looking at films. Instead, influenced by writers like Foucault, film theory has paralleled the theory of the left in general; there is no single reality; the meaning of a film, or a 'text' (to use the lingo) is in the arrangement of the 'signs', not in their relationship to the world they inhabit. Sparks writes:

So far as is yet evident in film theory, the consequence of this has been that, more or less, 'anything goes'. There is no longer any theoretical ground for deciding that one mode of inquiry or analytical system is to be preferred to any other and therefore all seem to have equal status.[21]

Thus film theory is as impressionistic and variable as the opinions of popular movie reviewers. It isn't clear how the insight an individual commentator might have on a particular film is because of, or in spite of, their theory of film.

As Richard Maltby and Ian Craven's *Hollywood Cinema* argues, Structuralist film criticism 'could explain neither how the texts themselves came into being as the result of a particular mode of production in Hollywood, nor what the wider relationship between those texts and the culture for which they were produced might have been'.[22] Nevertheless, as Sparks points out, the influence of the 1960s on film criticism also produced some useful results. The influence of feminism on film theory helped produce a greater scrutiny of Hollywood and the way it has portrayed women. Molly Haskell's *From Reverence to Rape*, written in the early 1970s, is one of the first and most readable accounts of the sexist portrayal of women in Hollywood films.[23] (Chapter 5 of Susan Faludi's *Backlash* is a brilliant chapter on how the 1980s backlash against women's rights was reflected in Hollywood films.[24])

Hollywood Cinema, in addition to being a good overview of the industry and how films get made, has a good chapter introducing the basic ideas of film theory. Especially good are its criticisms of the elitism in film theory, which has tended to see the viewer of the film as being passively shaped by the film rather than interacting with it. The view that Hollywood is a manufacturer of the dominant ideas, and the ignorant masses who view them are unwitting dupes, both overestimates Hollywood's role in shaping consciousness and underestimates the contradictory consciousness that people bring to watching films. As the authors write, 'The dominant ideology, however, is only dominant; it never succeeds in being totalising'.[25] Finally, V F Perkins' *Film as Film*, is a very short and accessible analysis of the narrative (mostly Hollywood) film.[26]

In the final analysis, it doesn't do much good to read about films unless you watch them. There is no substitute for seeing a *Battleship Potemkin*, a *Citizen Kane*, or a complete send up of the bourgeoisie like Luis Buñuel's *Exterminating Angel*, a surrealist film about a bunch of rich people who come to believe that they are trapped inside a mansion after they attend a party there, even though there is nothing preventing them from leaving. The best complement I have found in helping to look beyond the immediate impressions a film conveys to looking at how and why a film has the effect it does is in books which take a particular filmmaker and dissect his or her work.

I will recommend two. The first is Donald Spoto's *The Art of Alfred Hitchcock*, which reviews all of Hitchcock's major films, managing to artfully combine the analysis of form and content in Hitchcock's films.[27] Probably the most fun book I've read about film is *Hitchcock-Truffaut: A*

Definitive study of Alfred Hitchcock by Francois Truffaut, which consists of a series of interviews of Hitchcock by the French director.[28] This book helps answer questions like what devices and mannerisms films employ through editing, lighting, music, shot composition and so on, to convey their idea or message.

Two other books of interviews are worth reading to get an idea of the opinions and ideas of writers and directors themselves on filmmaking. *The Cineaste Interviews on the Art and Politics of the Cinema* has a series of interviews spanning the 1960s, 1970s and early 1980s with left wing and independent filmmakers like Costa-Gavras (director of films like *Z* and *Missing*), John Sayles (*Matewan*), and John Howard Lawson, founder of the Screen Writers Guild in Hollywood and a member of the Hollywood 10 who served time in gaol for bucking the House un-American Activities Committee in 1947.[29] A good follow up to that, *Reel Conversations*, contains interviews conducted in the early 1990s with, among others, Martin Scorsese, Michael Cimino, Oliver Stone, Francis Coppola, David Lynch and David Cronenberg.[30]

The popular American film critic Roger Ebert published a book in 1991 called *The Future of the Movies*, with interviews with George Lucas, Stephen Spielberg and Martin Scorsese. While I would not otherwise recommend it as important reading—the questions asked of the three directors are far too limited, the conclusion by Ebert's film critic sidekick Gene Siskel is worth quoting here:

> *In a fine 1979 book called **The Movie Brats**, Michael Pye and Lynda Myles profiled six filmmakers who were among the first wave of film school gradu-ates and who had come to prominence in the 1970s... The authors argued that the film revolution these directors participated in grew out of social changes in the culture itself. That makes sense. And so, believing that the past is prelude, if you want my prediction about the future of the movies, I believe things will not get better or more exciting until we have some good old-fashioned upheaval in this country and the world beyond.*[31]

Notes

Unfortunately, some of the books I refer to here are not in print, and some are in print in more recent editions than the ones I cite.

1 L Trotsky, *Problems of Everyday Life* (Pathfinder, 1973), p32.
2 Y Barna, *Eisenstein: The Growth of a Cinematic Genius* (Little Brown, 1973).
3 L Halliwell, *Halliwell's Film Guide, Fifth Edition* (Scribners, 1986), p183; *Halliwell's Filmgoers' Companion* (Scribners, 1984).
4 G Mast and B Kawin, *A Short History of the Movies* (Macmillan, 1992).
5 R Sklar, *Movie-Made America: A Cultural History of American Movies* (Vintage, 1994).

6   Ibid, p105.
7   T Shatz, *The Genius of the System: Hollywood Filmmaking in the Studio Era* (Pantheon, 1988).
8   V S Navasky, *Naming Names* (Penguin, 1991).
9   N L Schwartz, *Hollywood Writers' Wars* (Knopf, 1982).
10 B Neve, *Film and Politics in America: A Social Tradition* (Routledge, 1992).
11 M Pye and L Myles, *The Movie Brats: How the Film Generation Took Over Hollywood* (Holt Rinehart Winston, 1979).
12 S Bach, *Final Cut: Dreams and Disaster in the Making of **Heaven's Gate*** (Morrow, 1985).
13 T Shatz, 'The New Hollywood', from Collins, Radner, Preacher Collins (eds), *Film Theory Goes to the Movies* (Routledge, 1993).
14 A Vogel, *Film as a Subversive Art* (Random House, 1974), p32.
15 L and J Schnitzer and M Martin (eds), *Cinema in Revolution* (Hill and Wang, 1973).
16 Y Barna, op cit, p123.
17 S Eisenstein, *Film Form: Essays in Film Theory* (Harvest, 1949).
18 A Vogel, op cit, p36.
19 Mast and Cohen, eds, *Film Theory and Criticism: Introductory Reading* (Oxford, 1974).
20 C Sparks, 'A Marxist Guide to Contemporary Film Criticism', *International Socialism* 34.
21 Ibid, p95.
22 R Maltby and I Craven, *Hollywood Cinema* (Blackwell, 1995), p424.
23 M Haskell, *From Reverence to Rape: The Treatment of Women in the Movies* (Holt, 1973).
24 S Faludi, *Backlash* (Crown, 1991).
25 R Maltby and I Craven, op cit, p456.
26 V F Perkins, *Film as Film* (Pelican, 1972).
27 D Spoto, *The Art of Alfred Hitchcock* (Hopkinson and Blake, 1986).
28 F Truffaut, *Hitchcock-Truffaut: A Definitive Study of Alfred Hitchcock* (Touchstone, 1967).
29 D Georgakis and L Rubenstein (eds), *The Cineaste Interviews* (Lakeview Press, 1983).
30 G Nickenlooper, *Reel Conversations* (Citadel, 1991).
31 R Ebert and G Siskel, *The Future of the Movies* (Andrew and McMeel, 1991), p116.

The Socialist Workers Party is one of an international grouping of socialist organisations:

AUSTRALIA: International Socialists, GPO Box 1473N,
Melbourne 3001

BELGIUM: Socialisme International, 80 Rue Bois Gotha, 4000 Liège

BRITAIN: Socialist Workers Party, PO Box 82, London E3

CANADA: International Socialists, PO Box 339, Station E, Toronto,
Ontario M6H 4E3

CYPRUS: Ergatiki Demokratia, PO Box 7280, Nicosia

DENMARK: Internationale Socialister, Postboks 642, 2200
København N

FRANCE: Socialisme International, BP 189, 75926 Paris Cedex 19

GERMANY: Sozialistische Arbeitergruppe, Postfach 180367, 60084
Frankfurt 1

GREECE: Organosi Sosialisliki Epanastasi, c/o Workers Solidarity,
PO Box 8161, Athens 100 10

HOLLAND: International Socialists, PO Box 9720, 3506 GR Utrecht

IRELAND: Socialist Workers Party, PO Box 1648, Dublin 8

NEW ZEALAND:
International Socialist Organization, PO Box 6157,
Dunedin

NORWAY: Internasjonale Socialisterr, Postboks 5370, Majorstua,
0304 Oslo 3

POLAND: Solidarność Socjalistyczna, PO Box 12,
01-900 Warszawa 118

SOUTH AFRICA:
International Socialists of South Africa, PO Box 18530,
Hillbrow 2038, Johannesburg

UNITED STATES:
International Socialist Organisation, PO Box 16085,
Chicago, Illinois 60616

ZIMBABWE:
International Socialists, PO Box 6758, Harare

The following issues of *International Socialism* (second series) are available price £3.00 (including postage) from IS Journal, PO Box 82, London E3 3LH. *International Socialism* 2:58 and 2:65 are available on cassette from the Royal National Institute for the Blind (Peterborough Library Unit), Tel 01733 370777.

International Socialism 2:67 Summer 1995

Paul Foot: When will the Blair bubble burst? ★ Chris Harman: From Bernstein to Blair—100 years of revisionism ★ Chris Bambery: Was the Second World War a war for democracy? ★ Chris Nineham: Is the media all powerful? ★ Peter Morgan: How the West was won ★ Charlie Hore: Bookwatch: China since Mao ★

International Socialism 2:66 Spring 1995

Dave Crouch: The crisis in Russia and the rise of the right ★ Phil Gasper: Cruel and unusual punishment: the politics of crime in the United States ★ Alex Callinicos: Backwards to liberalism ★ John Newsinger: Matewan: film and working class struggle ★ John Rees: the light and the dark ★ Judy Cox: how to make the Tories disappear ★ Charlie Hore: Jazz: a reply to the critics ★ Pat Riordan: Bookwatch: Ireland ★

International Socialism 2:65 Special issue

Lindsey German: Frederick Engels: life of a revolutionary ★ John Rees: Engels' Marxism ★ Chris Harman: Engels and the origins of human society ★ Paul McGarr: Engels and natural science ★

International Socialism 2:64 Autumn 1994

Chris Harman: The prophet and the proletariat ★ Kieran Allen: What is changing in Ireland ★ Mike Haynes: The wrong road on Russia ★ Rob Ferguson: Hero and villain ★ Jane Elderton: Suffragette style ★ Chris Nineham: Two faces of modernism ★ Mike Hobart, Dave Harker and Matt Kelly: Three replies to 'Jazz—a people's music?' ★ Charlie Kimber: Bookwatch: South Africa—the struggle continues ★

International Socialism 2:63 Summer 1994

Alex Callinicos: Crisis and class struggle in Europe today ★ Duncan Blackie: The United Nations and the politics of imperialism ★ Brian Manning: The English Revolution and the transition from feudalism to capitalism ★ Lee Sustar: The roots of multi-racial labour unity in the United States ★ Peter Linebaugh: Days of villainy: a reply to two critics ★ Dave Sherry: Trotsky's last, greatest struggle ★ Peter Morgan: Geronimo and the end of the Indian wars ★ Dave Beecham: Ignazio Silone and *Fontamara* ★ Chris Bambery: Bookwatch: understanding fascism ★

International Socialism 2:62 Spring 1994

Sharon Smith: Mistaken identity—or can identity politics liberate the oppressed? ★ Iain Ferguson: Containing the crisis—crime and the Tories ★ John Newsinger: Orwell and the Spanish Revolution ★ Chris Harman: Change at the first millenium ★ Adrian Budd: Nation and empire—Labour's foreign policy 1945-51 ★ Gareth Jenkins: Novel questions ★ Judy Cox: Blake's revolution ★ Derek Howl: Bookwatch: the Russian Revolution ★

International Socialism 2:61 Winter 1994

Lindsey German: Before the flood? ★ John Molyneux: The 'politically correct' controversy ★ David McNally: E P Thompson—class struggle and historical materialism ★ Charlie Hore: Jazz—a people's music ★ Donny Gluckstein: Revolution and the challenge of labour ★ Charlie Kimber: Bookwatch: the Labour Party in decline ★

International Socialism 2:60 Autumn 1993

Chris Bambery: Euro-fascism: the lessons of the past and present tasks ★ Chris Harman: Where is capitalism going? (part 2) ★ Mike Gonzalez: Chile and the struggle for workers' power ★ Phil Marshall: Bookwatch: Islamic activism in the Middle East ★

International Socialism 2:59 Summer 1993

Ann Rogers: Back to the workhouse ★ Kevin Corr and Andy Brown: The labour aristocracy and the roots of reformism ★ Brian Manning: God, Hill and Marx ★ Henry Maitles: Cutting the wire: a criticial appraisal of Primo Levi ★ Hazel Croft: Bookwatch: women and work ★

International Socialism 2:58 Spring 1993

Chris Harman: Where is capitalism going? (part one) ★ Ruth Brown and Peter Morgan: Politics and the class struggle today: a roundtable discussion ★ Richard Greeman: The return of Comrade Tulayev: Victor Serge and the tragic vision of Stalinism ★ Norah Carlin: A new English revolution ★ John Charlton: Building a new world ★ Colin Barker: A reply to Dave McNally ★

International Socialism 2:57 Winter 1992
Lindsey German: Can there be a revolution in Britain? ★ Mike Haynes: Columbus, the Americas and the rise of capitalism ★ Mike Gonzalez: The myths of Columbus: a history ★ Paul Foot: Poetry and revolution ★ Alex Callinicos: Rhetoric which cannot conceal a bankrupt theory: a reply to Ernest Mandel ★ Charlie Kimber: Capitalism, cruelty and conquest ★ David McNulty: Comments on Colin Barker's review of Thompson's *Customs in Common* ★

International Socialism 2:56 Autumn 1992
Chris Harman: The Return of the National Question ★ Dave Treece: Why the Earth Summit failed ★ Mike Gonzalez: Can Castro survive? ★ Lee Humber and John Rees: The good old cause—an interview with Christopher Hill ★ Ernest Mandel: The Impasse of Schematic Dogmatism ★

International Socialism 2:55 Summer 1992
Alex Callinicos: Race and class ★ Lee Sustar: Racism and class struggle in the American Civil War era ★ Lindsey German and Peter Morgan: Prospects for socialists—an interview with Tony Cliff ★ Robert Service: Did Lenin lead to Stalin? ★ Samuel Farber: In defence of democratic revolutionary socialism ★ David Finkel: Defending 'October' or sectarian dogmatism? ★ Robin Blackburn: Reply to John Rees ★ John Rees: Dedicated followers of fashion ★ Colin Barker: In praise of custom ★ Sheila McGregor: Revolutionary witness ★

International Socialism 2:54 Spring 1992
Sharon Smith: Twilight of the American dream ★ Mike Haynes: Class and crisis—the transition in eastern Europe ★ Costas Kossis: A miracle without end? Japanese capitalism and the world economy ★ Alex Callinicos: Capitalism and the state system: A reply to Nigel Harris ★ Steven Rose: Do animals have rights? ★ John Charlton: Crime and class in the 18th century ★ John Rees: Revolution, reform and working class culture ★ Chris Harman: Blood simple ★

International Socialism 2:52 Autumn 1991
John Rees: In defence of October ★ Ian Taylor and Julie Waterson: The political crisis in Greece—an interview with Maria Styllou and Panos Garganas ★ Paul McGarr: Mozart, overture to revolution ★ Lee Humber: Class, class consciousness and the English Revolution ★ Derek Howl: The legacy of Hal Draper ★

International Socialism 2:51 Summer 1991
Chris Harman: The state and capitalism today ★ Alex Callinicos: The end of nationalism? ★ Sharon Smith: Feminists for a strong state? ★ Colin Sparks and Sue Cockerill: Goodbye to the Swedish miracle ★ Simon Phillips: The South African Communist Party and the South African working class ★ John Brown: Class conflict and the crisis of feudalism ★

International Socialism 2:49 Winter 1990
Chris Bambery: The decline of the Western Communist Parties ★ Ernest Mandel: A theory which has not withstood the test of time ★ Chris Harman: Criticism which does not withstand the test of logic ★ Derek Howl: The law of value In the USSR ★ Terry Eagleton: Shakespeare and the class struggle ★ Lionel Sims: Rape and pre-state societies ★ Sheila McGregor: A reply to Lionel Sims ★

International Socialism 2:48 Autumn 1990
Lindsey German: The last days of Thatcher ★ John Rees: The new imperialism ★ Neil Davidson and Donny Gluckstein: Nationalism and the class struggle in Scotland ★ Paul McGarr: Order out of chaos ★

International Socialism 2:46 Winter 1989
Chris Harman: The storm breaks ★ Alex Callinicos: Can South Africa be reformed? ★ John Saville: Britain, the Marshall Plan and the Cold War ★ Sue Clegg: Against the stream ★ John Rees: The rising bourgeoisie ★

International Socialism 2:44 Autumn 1989
Charlie Hore: China: Tiananmen Square and after ★ Sue Clegg: Thatcher and the welfare state ★ John Molyneux: *Animal Farm* revisited ★ David Finkel: After Arias, is the revolution over? ★ John Rose: Jews in Poland ★

International Socialism 2:43 Summer 1989 (Reprint—special price £4.50)
Marxism and the Great French Revolution by Paul McGarr and Alex Callinicos

International Socialism 2:42 Spring 1989
Chris Harman: The myth of market socialism ★ Norah Carlin: Roots of gay oppression ★ Duncan Blackie: Revolution in science ★ International Socialism Index ★

International Socialism 2:41 Winter 1988
Polish socialists speak out: Solidarity at the Crossroads ★ Mike Haynes: Nightmares of the market ★ Jack Robertson: Socialists and the unions ★ Andy Strouthous: Are the unions in decline? ★ Richard Bradbury: What is Post-Structuralism? ★ Colin Sparks: George Bernard Shaw ★

International Socialism 2:39 Summer 1988
Chris Harman and Andy Zebrowski: Glasnost, before the storm ★ Chanie Rosenberg: Labour and the fight against fascism ★ Mike Gonzalez: Central America after the Peace Plan ★ Ian Birchall: Raymond Williams ★ Alex Callinicos: Reply to John Rees ★

International Socialism 2:35 Summer 1987
Pete Green: Capitalism and the Thatcher years ★ Alex Callinicos: Imperialism, capitalism and the state today ★ Ian Birchall: Five years of *New Socialist* ★ Callinicos and Wood debate 'Looking for alternatives to reformism' ★ David Widgery replies on 'Beating Time' ★

International Socialism 2:31 Winter 1985
Alex Callinicos: Marxism and revolution In South Africa ★ Tony Cliff: The tragedy of A J Cook ★ Nigel Harris: What to do with London? The strategies of the GLC ★

International Socialism 2:30 Autumn 1985
Gareth Jenkins: Where is the Labour Party heading? ★ David McNally: Debt, inflation and the rate of profit ★ Ian Birchall: The terminal crisis in the British Communist Party ★ replies on Women's oppression and *Marxism Today* ★

International Socialism 2:29 Summer 1985
Special issue on the class struggle and the left in the aftermath of the miners' defeat ★ Tony Cliff: Patterns of mass strike ★ Chris Harman: 1984 and the shape of things to come ★ Alex Callinicos: The politics of *Marxism Today* ★

International Socialism 2:26 Spring 1985
Pete Green: Contradictions of the American boom ★ Colin Sparks: Labour and imperialism ★ Chris Bambery: Marx and Engels and the unions ★ Sue Cockerill: The municipal road to socialism ★ Norah Carlin: Is the family part of the superstructure? ★ Kieran Allen: James Connolly and the 1916 rebellion ★

International Socialism 2:25 Autumn 1984
John Newsinger: Jim Larkin, Syndicalism and the 1913 Dublin Lockout ★ Pete Binns: Revolution and state capitalism in the Third World ★ Colin Sparks: Towards a police state? ★ Dave Lyddon: Demystifying the downturn ★ John Molyneux: Do working class men benefit from women's oppression? ★

International Socialism 2:18 Winter 1983
Donny Gluckstein: Workers' councils in Western Europe ★ Jane Ure Smith: The early Communist press in Britain ★ John Newsinger: The Bolivian Revolution ★ Andy Durgan: Largo Caballero and Spanish socialism ★ M Barker and A Beezer: Scarman and the language of racism ★

International Socialism 2:14 Winter 1981
Chris Harman: The riots of 1981 ★ Dave Beecham: Class struggle under the Tories ★ Tony Cliff: Alexandra Kollontai ★ L James and A Paczuska: Socialism needs feminism ★ reply to Cliff on Zetkin ★ Feminists In the labour movement ★

International Socialism 2:13 Summer 1981
Chris Harman: The crisis last time ★ Tony Cliff: Clara Zetkin ★ Ian Birchall: Left Social Democracy In the French Popular Front ★ Pete Green: Alternative Economic Strategy ★ Tim Potter: The death of Eurocommunism ★

International Socialism 2:12 Spring 1981
Jonathan Neale: The Afghan tragedy ★ Lindsey German: Theories of patriarchy ★ Ray Challinor: McDouall and Physical Force Chartism ★ S Freeman & B Vandesteeg: Unproductive labour ★ Alex Callinicos: Wage labour and capitalism ★ Italian fascism ★ Marx's theory of history ★ Cabral ★

International Socialism 2:11 Winter 1980
Rip Bulkeley et al: CND In the 50s ★ Marx's theory of crisis and its critics ★ Andy Durgan: Revolutionary anarchism in Spain ★ Alex Callinicos: Politics or abstract thought ★ Fascism in Europe ★ Marilyn Monroe ★